FREE PUBLIC LIBRARY
DALTON, MASSACHUSETTS

First opened, May 1861   Accepted by Town, March 1885

LIBRARY RULES

1. A fine of 5c a day will be charged for each adult book kept overtime beyond the due date; for Juvenile and Young People's books, the fine will be 1c a day for each book.
2. Full value must be paid if a book is LOST; a reasonable fine if it is damaged.
3. No books or other library materials may be borrowed by persons with a record of unreturned materials and unpaid fines or losses. However, use of the reading rooms and reference and advisory service are always available to everybody.

Please note that all materials may have the due date extended, either by phone or in person, unless a reserve for same is on file, or a 7 day book.

The Romance of
Casco Bay

ALSO BY EDWARD ROWE SNOW

THE ROMANCE OF CASCO BAY

Edward Rowe Snow

Illustrated

DODD, MEAD & COMPANY · NEW YORK

Library of Congress Cataloging in Publication Data

Snow, Edward Rowe.
    The romance of Casco Bay.

    Includes bibliographical references and index.
    1. Casco Bay region, Me.—History. 2. Casco Bay
region, Me.—Description and travel. 3. Canoes and
canoeing—Casco Bay, Me. 4. Snow, Edward Rowe.
I. Title.
F27.C3S63   974.1'91   75–29352
ISBN 0–396–07214–3

To Johanna von Tiling and
Peter McLaughlin of Casco Bay

INTRODUCTION

For many years I have been gathering information and unusual stories on Casco Bay, its islands, lighthouses, ledges, treasure hunts, ghosts, and the coastline itself. I have traveled 339 miles by canoe in Casco Bay, flown over the region for forty-one years, and made trips there in lobster boats, cabin cruisers, and almost every passenger craft that has run on the Casco Bay Lines for the past generation.

After years of research the manuscript of this book ran almost eighteen hundred pages. For reasons of space it was necessary to eliminate much that should have been included. In the material that was finally selected, I have attempted to steer a strict course as did sailors of old between the legendary Scylla and Charybdis to avoid the rocks of error and the whirlpools of historical confusion.

I thank the members of the Portland Bicentennial Committee for their help. The Maine Historical Society and the State Library of Augusta were also most helpful.

Individuals who gave me substantial assistance include the

following: Neal W. Allen, Dorothy Snow Bicknell, Laura Ann Bicknell, Richard Carlisle, Frederick G. S. Clow, David Coyle, Arthur Cunningham, Maryann Damon, James Douglas, Walter Spahr Ehrenfeld, E. Marie Estes, Jean Foley, Suzanne Flandreau, Marie Hansen, Z. William Hawk, Melina Herron, Elizabeth Darling Jackson, Glenn D. Jackson, Joseph Kolb, Robert W. Laughlin, Captain Robert A. Lee, William L. MacVane, Jr., Peter McLaughlin, Larry Molignano, John E. Menario, Robert E. Moody, Richard Nakashian, Joel O'Brien, Doris P. Olney, Beth Palmer, William Pyne, H. A. C. Rauchfuss, George B. Richardson, Elizabeth Ring, Elva Ruiz, Helen Salkowski, Frederick Sanford, Chester Shea, Alfred Schroeder, James C. Simmons, William Smitz, Donald B. Snow, Vernon A. Stevenson, Barbara Hayward Urbanowitz, Johanna E. R. von Tiling, Susan Williams.

I am deeply indebted to John R. Herbert, prominent Quincy resident and newsman, for his valuable assistance down through the years.

My wife Anna-Myrle, patient and helpful, has now assisted me on several score books, and deserves my love and deepest admiration.

I offer my thanks at this time to the scores of others who have assisted me in the writing of this book, and remind my readers that many of the chapters which could not crowd themselves into this volume will be included in a later work.

EDWARD ROWE SNOW
Marshfield, Massachusetts

Contents

PART ONE

Lighthouses and Forts

1

Portland Head Light

Portland Head and its light seem to symbolize the state of Maine—rocky coast, breaking waves, sparkling water, and clear, pure air. Built on the headland for which the city was named—the promontory was known as Portland Head as early as 1750—this beautiful lighthouse has been admired by thousands of visitors. People from all states of the Union have made the journey to the rocky cliffs at the entrance to Portland Harbor to see this patriarch of all Maine lighthouses. The great white tower stands against the sky, with its identifying ridge built out from the flush sides of the stone edifice two thirds of the distance to the top.

Many outstanding Maine writers and poets have visited Portland Head Light through the years, but to me Portland Light has always stood for Longfellow. Whenever I am fortunate enough to be at Portland Head, I like to reserve a few important moments to go out to the rock where Longfellow often sat as he planned his verses. Perhaps it was there that the immortal lines that follow first came to his mind:

I remember the black wharves, and the slips,
   And the sea-tides tossing free;
And Spanish sailors with bearded lips,
And the beauty and mystery of the ships,
   And the magic of the sea.

The construction of Portland Head Light began in 1787 under the supervision of the commonwealth of Massachusetts, of which Maine was then a part. Taken over by the federal government, the lighthouse was finished under the direction of John Nichols and Jonathan Bryant. By 1790 the edifice had reached a height of fifty-eight feet and was considered finished. When the officials climbed to the top of the tower, however, they found that a neighboring headland unfortunately shut out the view in one direction entirely, and decided that additional height would have to be given the tower. Authority to raise the tower finally came from Alexander Hamilton, Secretary of the Treasury.

The original lantern was planned to be fairly large, but because of the sloping sides and extra height of the tower, the reduced area at the top was too small for the lantern the authorities had chosen to install. Finally, a smaller lantern was obtained, and the lighthouse was finished without further delay.

Many nautically inclined citizens of Portland were eager to be appointed as keeper of the new lighthouse, but the choice finally narrowed down to two individuals, Captain Joseph Greenleaf and Barzillai Delano. Greenleaf was recommended by Portland's collector, Nathaniel F. Fosdick, on November 2, 1790, while Delano was the choice of two of the committeemen who arranged for the construction of the tower.

Captain Joseph Greenleaf won the appointment, receiving official notice from George Washington himself in a letter written on January 7, 1791. Although Greenleaf was the first keeper, when his career ended after a few years at Portland

Head, Barzillai Delano was waiting for the position and it was given to him.

A few years after the tower was built, it was found to be damp and uncomfortable. General Benjamin Lincoln, Massachusetts Lighthouse Superintendent, suggested as a remedy that pine planks could be used to enclose the walls of the lighthouse, after which three or four iron hoops could secure the planks to the stone walls of the tower itself. A good coat of shingles, "well painted," according to Lincoln, would complete the unusual plan, which, as far as is known, was never carried out.

General Henry Dearborn visited Portland Head Light in the fall of 1810 and interviewed Keeper Delano about repairing the sagging structure. The flooring was rotting away, and it was decided that new timbers were necessary. When the carpenter arrived to make the repairs, he found that Delano had stored practically the entire year's supply of oil in the room where the alterations were to be made and it reached almost to the ceiling. The lighthouse keeper was afraid the whole building might collapse if the heavy weight of oil were shifted. Nothing further was attempted that year, and the carpenter returned the following summer to make his repairs.

When a sea captain made a complaint about Portland Head Light to Tench Coxe, Commissioner of the Revenue at the capital in Philadelphia, Benjamin Lincoln made a thorough investigation. The captain stated that he had been unable to see the light while approaching the harbor. Lincoln's investigation revealed that there was no method of ventilation in the tower to carry off the smoke so that quite often the tubes of glass were heavily coated over. Lincoln then explained to Commissioner Coxe that that the diameter at the top of the tower had been reduced to a little less than six feet because of the extra height needed to clear the nearby headland, but in spite of this, "there is room enough to burn almost any quantity of oil and yet if the lamps are properly arranged space enough to clean the glass."

Lincoln was doubtful that the lamps were as weak as claimed. He was "a little surprized if the Lights are badly kept that no Master of Vessell should have hinted it to me. They are every week at this Office and often two or three in a week." He also expressed the hope that politics was not entering into the matter.

An oil shed was built out of doors, and also a cistern, which was protected from the spray by a rock fence. The expense of these tasks was considered high, $179.07, but according to Lincoln, the people of Portland "would not perform it for less."

In 1820, when the state of Maine was set off from its mother, Massachusetts, the new state received local jurisdiction over its lighthouses, with supervision from Washington, of course. Portland Head Light thus received a new supervisor, Isaac Ilsley of Portland. The letter announcing the change to Collector Henry A. S. Dearborn of Boston follows:

> Treasury Department, Fifth Auditor's Office
> March 29, 1820
>
> Sir,
>
> As the district of Maine has been admitted into the union as an independent state, its relation to the United States has undergone a change which renders it proper that the several offices of the United States within it should be confided to its citizens. The superintendence of the Light House establishment, therefore, with which you have heretofore been charged, within the limits of that state, has been transferred to Isaac Ilsley, Esq., the Collector of the Customs at Portland. There was the less repugnance to the change, as the emoluments, contrasted with the duties to be performed, could not, it is believed, be an object with you to retain the trust in your hands. Your agency in regard to the Light House establishment will consequently be confined to Massachusetts Proper.

You will be pleased to communicate to Mr. Ilsley such information relative to the charge now committed to him as you shall think of advantage, and to instruct the several Keepers of Light Houses within the state of Maine to make all necessary communications and returns to him.

I am vt.

S. Pleasonton

Fifth Auditor and Acting Commissioner
of the Revenue

Henry A. S. Dearborn, Esq.

The long career of Keeper Delano at Portland Head Light came to an end in 1820, when he died in service at the lighthouse. The new keeper was Joshua Freeman, as the following letter reveals:

Treasury Department, Fifth Auditor's Office
July 3, 1820

Sir:—

I have to inform you that the President has appointed Joshua Freeman to be keeper of the Light House on Portland Head, in the room of Barzillai Delano, deceased, of which you will be pleased to give him notice.

I am vt.

S. Pleasonton

Fifth Auditor and Acting Commissioner
of the Rev.

Isaac Ilsley Esq.

Three decades later, when representatives of the newly commissioned Lighthouse Board visited Portland Head on July 5, 1852, John F. Watts was keeper. He told the board members that when he became keeper no one could tell him how to operate the light, so he was forced to hire a man for two days to teach him how to do it. He pointed out that the reflectors, less than two years old, were badly scratched. The members of the board were surprised to find that the keeper's foghorn was blown only in accordance with private arrangement with certain steamers. Keeper Watts lived in a dwelling house which was in very poor condition, and the lighthouse itself was being undermined by rats.

As a result of the Lighthouse Board's report, as well as considerable criticism from the Portland shipmasters, a Fresnal lens was installed in 1855, the private foghorn was replaced by a regular fog bell operated in bad weather for all shipping, and necessary repairs were made at the base of the tower.

During the Civil War, raids on shipping in and out of Portland Harbor became almost commonplace. Because of the necessity for ships at sea to sight Portland Head Light as soon as possible, it was agreed that the edifice should be raised even higher. After the war ended, the tower was increased in height by eight feet, and a new set of lenses was installed.

The September Gale of 1869, which left its mark at so many other lighthouses and lifesaving stations along the coast, did not spare Portland Head. The storm ripped the great fog bell from its fastening and hurled it into a nearby gully. A new fog bell tower was built in 1870 with a Stevens striker, but the bell was soon replaced by a Daboll trumpet which had seen service at Monhegan Island. In 1872 a second-class trumpet replaced the Monhegan signal, and in 1887 Boston Light's old twenty-four-inch caloric engine was installed at Portland Head.

In 1883 Portland Head Light had been lowered twenty feet, only to be raised twenty feet the following year. No one seems to be able to explain these changes. Finally, in 1885, Portland Head Light was made a second-order station by enlarging the tower at the top and putting a more powerful lens in place. The new light was first illuminated on January 15, 1885.

Portland Head Light in peacetime is an occulting white light.

The light flashes, then it occults, or goes through a period of darkness, before the next flash. Every two seconds of the night the beam of light is seen from its tower 101 feet in the air. Usually during wartime the light is turned out, but in the summer of 1945 it was again lighted.

Many important lighthouse keepers have had tours of duty at Maine's oldest beacon. Keeper Joshua Strout was a member of a family that served at Portland Head Light Station for almost sixty years. In 1867 Joshua F. Strout as head keeper received $620 a year, while his wife, May, earned $480 as assistant keeper. When Strout retired, his son Joseph W. Strout took his place. Joseph Strout remained at Portland Head more than half a century, and was dearly loved by all who knew him.

Frank O. Hilt then became keeper. Behind the tower he built an enormous checkerboard, each square almost a foot in size, with checkers weighing several pounds each. One of my most delightful memories of Portland Head Light is that of my wife, Anna-Myrle, and Keeper Hilt playing checkers on the huge board. I photographed Keeper Hilt, who in his prime was a 300-pound giant, from the top of the tower as Mrs. Snow contemplated a move on the great checkerboard below.

Robert Thayer Sterling, Hilt's able assistant, became the head keeper when Hilt retired. Sterling wrote a delightful book which has become a treasured volume, *Lighthouses of the Maine Coast.*

Other subsequent keepers include William L. Lockhart, William T. Burns, and Earle E. Benson, Benson taking command in 1952.

When I flew my thirty-eighth annual Flying Santa mission to the lighthouses last Christmas, I was forced to pass over Portland Head Light in a blinding snowstorm, landing minutes later at Portland Airport in five inches of snow. A young coast-guardsman, Brian Belanger from the South Portland Base, transported the more than twenty packages I had planned to drop over the Maine lighthouses to the base, and they were delivered at the lonely islands in time for Christmas. In each package is enclosed a self-addressed postcard, and a few days later I received the card from Portland Head's lighthouse keeper, B. M. Cavanaugh.

If you sail out beyond Portland Head, you can barely make out the white rock where Henry Wadsworth Longfellow sat so often when he was composing his poetry. Possibly the first thoughts of the following lines came to him at Portland Head:

> And as the evening darkens, lo! how bright
> Through the deep purple of the twilight air,
> Beams forth the sudden radiance of its light
> With strange unearthly splendour in its glare!
>
> And the great ships sail outward and return
> Bending and blowing o'er the billowy swells;
> And ever joyful, as they see it burn
> They wave their silent welcomes and farewells.

2

The Cape Elizabeth Lights

Though the Old Two Lights may send no more
    Their twin beams through the dark—
No more shine through the murky night,
    On schooner, sloop, and barque,

Yet still a quenchless beacon burns
    On the headland, as of yore,
And a cautioning call forever turns
    The vessels from the shore.

"Old Anthony" sends forth his voice,
    And the wheeling seagulls hear,
While Half-way Rock gives back the sound,
    And the dipping coasters veer.

And the tides that turn on Trundy's Reef,
    Ram Island, and Seguin,
Still swing the ships toward Portland Head,
    Where the lighthouse guides them in.

Thus did gifted poet Sylvia Tryon express her thoughts some years ago when she realized that the Cape Elizabeth lighthouse property was being given up by the government.

A few months ago I was near the two lights and discovered that at Cape Elizabeth one can get into the mood to appreciate Homer's reference to the watch-fire's light, probably the first definite reference to this subject in literature. As I stood there near the two lights, I thought of the 250th Anniversary celebration of the initial lighting of the first beacon in America at Boston Light on September 14, 1716. Elliot Lee Richardson, now ambassador to England, stood with me in a little group, ready to speak on a rainy day.

As the heavens opened up, I took pity on the assemblage waiting in the downpour, and drastically reduced my speech until barely more than Homer's comments from the *Iliad* remained. Earlier I had mentioned to Elliot Richardson that as a student of classical Greek at college under Dr. Paul M. Adams I was never considered that teacher's greatest success. When my turn came, I sensed Richardson's presence near me. My fellow Harvardian had edged over to a position immediately behind my left shoulder in an attempt to give much-appreciated moral support as I began Homer's reference, possibly the first anywhere, to a beacon guiding a ship at sea:

ως δι οτ αν εκ ποντοιο σελας ναυτησι φανηη
καιομενοιο πυρος το δε καιεται υψοθ ορεσφιν
σταθμω εν οιοπολω

The English translation, for those of my readers who are no better at reading Greek than I am, follows:

When to seamen over the wave is carried the watch-fire's light which some shepherd kindles by his lonely fold, high in the hills.

Cape Elizabeth Lighthouse Station, located several miles to the southeast of the Pine Tree State's largest city, was built in 1828, and was declared by the government to be among the most important beacons on the East Coast. Actually, the light station is considerably higher than Boston Light.

In 1811 General Dearborn wrote to Secretary of the Treasury Gallatin that he had arranged to erect a monument or marker for the identification of Cape Elizabeth by ships at sea, and on June 3 of that year final plans were made to build a monument forty feet high with a twenty-foot base. But the daytime marker, of course, was not a guide to ships at night, and agitation gradually crystallized into the approval by Congress of the construction of a lighthouse at Cape Elizabeth. The orders eventually reached Stephen Pleasonton, fifth auditor of the treasury, under whose jurisdiction all lighthouses were erected at that time. In his letter of March 13, 1827, to Isaac Ilsley, who was in charge of Maine lighthouses, Pleasonton said in part:

Why two Light houses are to be placed upon this Cape, and so small a sum allowed for building them, I am uninformed. I must request you however to make an examination, or cause it to be made, and inform me whether two Light houses are necessary, and for what sum suitable buildings can be erected. You will also ascertain whether the sites can be obtained, and for what price.

I am,
S. Pleasonton

Fifteen months later the contract was awarded to the lowest bidder, Jeremiah Berry, who constructed the two rubble-stone towers for $4,250. Twelve acres of Cape Elizabeth land were purchased at the time.

During the construction of the towers, the local representative, Isaac Ilsley, visited the scene to superintend the workmen, and later included his own expenses in the accounts sent to Washington. Stephen Pleasonton took exception to the expense, saying that a commission of 2.5 percent was sufficient, and ended with the sentence, "You will therefore strike out of the account for Cape Elizabeth lighthouses the charge for superintendence of the workmen."

President John Quincy Adams appointed Elisha Jordan as the first keeper at Cape Elizabeth Lights in October, 1828. Jordan had been chosen from a list of eighteen candidates, including Josiah Waistcoat, Isaiah Snow, Amos Wormwell, and Alexander Goldthwait. Jordan's salary was placed at $450 a year, and he was instructed to reside at the station and make it a habit to be at home.

Mrs. Amelia D. Chamberlain, at the age of nineteen, became the assistant keeper at Cape Elizabeth. Mrs. Chamberlain would be a witness to the thrilling wreck of the steamer *Bohemian* in 1864. The next spring, on the death of Abraham Lincoln, she assisted in draping the lighthouse towers with black bunting.

The Fresnal lens had been installed at Cape Elizabeth Lights in 1855, making the lights brighter and more readily identified. Ten years later an unusual change was made for daytime recognition. The west tower was painted with one broad, vertical red stripe, and the east light was given four horizontal bands of red. It is believed no picture of this color combination is in existence. A giant steam whistle was installed on the station four years later for use in foggy weather, and this necessitated the construction of another separate building, some distance away from the keeper's home, for the installation of a huge boiler and other essential parts of the plant. The ten-inch locomotive whistle gave a terrific blast every minute lasting eight seconds.

In 1873 the rubble towers were taken down, and the next year two stately cast-iron edifices were erected in their place, three hundred yards apart. The characteristics of the two lights were then changed to one fixed and one flashing light, and a fog siren was installed to replace the locomotive whistle. A short time afterward the keeper's dwelling was repaired and a new house built for the head keeper. In 1884 a first-order mineral oil lamp was installed in the east tower by Keeper Marcus A. Hanna, who was the first to illuminate the new light. Hanna had been keeper at Pemaquid Point Light since 1869.

Perhaps the most thrilling episode in Cape Elizabeth history occurred on January 28, 1885, when Keeper Hanna saved two of the crew members of the schooner *Australia* of Boothbay, Maine. The weather had been fair but cold the day before, with a light wind blowing in from the northeast. Toward dusk the breeze freshened, and by midnight a severe storm swept in from the sea. Keeper Hanna, who had been sick with a bad cold, was doing his best to conquer his miserable feelings and make sure that the giant fog signal blast was operating at the height of its efficiency.

But his was a hopeless task. The wind increased, the snow fell in unprecedented heaviness, and the waves, although the tide was low, were soon smashing against the ledges around the headland. By three in the morning Keeper Hanna realized that no ship at sea could possibly hear the steam whistle, although he kept sounding the blasts every minute of the night. He felt very ill and tried to ward off an intense desire to sleep. Finally, at six in the morning, Assistant Keeper Hiram Staples reported at the fog signal house for Hanna's relief. By this time, according to Hanna, "one of the coldest and most violent storms of snow, wind, and vapor was raging that I ever witnessed."

When Hanna started back to his home from the fog station, he encountered great snowdrifts three to five feet high, and in his weakened condition had to crawl through the deeper drifts to reach his home. Hanna's wife was waiting for him, and after telling him that he should have known better than to go out on such a night, put him to bed, announcing that she would attend to putting out the lamp in the lighthouse at the proper time. Keeper Hanna, exhausted from his cold and his struggle through the deep snowdrifts, soon fell asleep.

Mrs. Hanna, as many other faithful wives have done in their unsung careers at lonely lighthouse stations, extinguished the lamp in the tower at twelve minutes past seven, near sunrise. On her return from the lighthouse she went out of doors on the lee side of the building, where there is a commanding view of the open sea. It was at twenty minutes before nine that she suddenly saw, through the snow and the vapor, the masts of a vessel loom up a quarter mile from shore. Mrs. Hanna rushed to her husband with the exciting but disheartening news. "There is a vessel ashore near the fog signal!"

Hastily leaving his bed, without a thought for himself, Keeper Marcus Hanna dressed at once and rushed out of the house. He floundered through the snowdrifts and soon reached the fog signal station, which was about two hundred yards from the wreck. Calling to Staples, Hanna found to his surprise that his assistant had not noticed the wreck.

The unfortunate vessel was the schooner *Australia*, which had sailed from Boothbay Harbor at five o'clock the evening before, bound for Boston. Captain J. W. Lewis had a crew of two men, Irving Pierce and William Kellar, both seamen. When the storm hit them off Halfway Rock Light at eleven o'clock that night, Captain Lewis had chosen to run for Portland, but later accepted the advice of Pierce to stand off instead. Shortly afterward the mainsail blew to pieces, and it was agreed to jog off and on under reefed foresail until morning. Because the temperature was down to four above zero, the *Australia* iced over so heavily that the crew were forced to throw over the deckload to keep the vessel afloat. At eight o'clock in the morning they saw Cape Elizabeth Lights, and hoisted the peak of the mainsail, trusting they could weather the cape.

The wind and sea, however, united to cause their disaster.

The *Australia* soon grounded on the ledge near the fog signal station, and the men aboard took to the rigging. Because of their frozen condition—they were heavily coated with ice—the men were unable to move. Suddenly Captain Lewis was hit by a great wave and washed off the shrouds down onto the deck. With his last bit of strength he managed to climb up again, but the battering he had received made him an easy victim for the next great billow which swept across the schooner. When the wave went down, his men saw him no more.

Seamen Pierce and Kellar clung to their places in the rigging. Each successive sea swept across them, leaving its thin coating of icy water which froze on their helpless bodies. Soon they were unable to move in any way, their ice-covered forms turning whiter every minute. The tide was coming higher and higher, and the schooner seemed doomed to break up.

Just as they were about to give up all hope, they saw Keeper Hanna and his assistant approaching. The two keepers had gone to a pilothouse nearby for a good line to throw out to the schooner. After securing a heavy iron weight to the end of the line, the keepers made their way down to the shore where the schooner was being pounded to pieces as the tide rose. The vessel had hit the beach, which runs northeast to southwest at this point, heading to the westward, so that her starboard side was near shore, perched at an angle of forty-five degrees with the land. In this position every sea would smash into the *Australia*'s stern, sweep high into the air until even the mastheads were hidden from view, and burst out over the bow and sides as it made its way toward shore.

Captain Hanna reached the ice-covered rocks near the schooner, and after getting a vantage point knee deep in the seething foam, made an attempt to throw the line aboard. The weight fell into the sea ten feet short of its goal. Again and again he tried to land the line aboard the schooner. Each time he hauled back the icy cord, it was stiff and unyielding to the touch, contact with the water having frozen it even in that short period of seconds. After at least twenty attempts the poor lighthouse keeper had to give up, for his feet and hands were wet and freezing, the spray was icing his clothing into boardlike garments which allowed him no freedom of motion, and his sick condition had left him weak. Assistant Hiram Staples had gone back to the fog signal station some time before, discouraged by the many futile attempts to reach the two freezing men aboard the *Australia*. Keeper Hanna decided to get ashore and exercise his body by stamping his feet and pounding his arms, and then return to the schooner for a last attempt. His wife, meanwhile, had aroused the neighbors. Help was on the way.

Suddenly, a towering wave, higher than all the rest, struck the schooner, lifted her bodily from the ledge, and smashed the *Australia* against the rocks nearer to the fog signal station. Her whole port side was stove in, and the *Australia* was now over on her beam ends. Keeper Hanna, hurrying to the shore, threw out his line and was overjoyed to watch it land aboard the schooner. The men, however, could not free themselves from the shrouds to which they were frozen, and the line slid off into the sea.

Hanna, shivering with the cold, now waded waist deep into the sea and made his final attempt. By this time Seaman Pierce was able to break away from the icy coating which enveloped him. The line dropped at the foot of the shrouds, and Pierce, with great effort, for his clothing had frozen stiff, slowly reached for the line, grasped it, and bent it around his waist.

Hanna realized that it would be almost impossible to pull the man in unaided, and cried desperately at the top of his voice for help. No one came, so he decided that he could wait no longer. Pierce signaled that he was ready, and went over the side into the sea. The lighthouse keeper hauled away. Wave after wave battered the frozen man as he was pulled to land. When he hit shore, Hanna was forced to pull him up over the rocky ledge.

Later Hanna said he never knew where he obtained the energy to pull and push the "helpless, frozen lump of humanity to a place out of reach of the surf." Irving Pierce was totally blind from exposure to the cold, and his jaws were frozen together. His whole appearance was ghastly. "The expression of his face," Hanna said later, "I shall not soon forget."

But there was still another shipwrecked mariner aboard the schooner, which was now going to pieces rapidly. Leaving Pierce for the moment, Keeper Hanna stumbled down to the shore again, adjusted the line, and made his throw. Floating wreckage fouled the line. He tried again and again, and finally reached Kellar, who wound it around his icy body and signaled at once for the pull ashore. Although he knew in his heart that he would not have strength enough to pull Kellar out of the ocean, Hanna answered that he was ready and told Kellar to jump into the ocean. The lighthouse keeper made a silent prayer that help would come in time, as his strength was failing fast.

As he began the torturous pull ashore, Keeper Hanna was greeted by shouts, and Assistant Staples, together with two neighbors, ran down the bank to help him. They had arrived just in time as if in answer to Hanna's prayer for aid. The four men soon had the helpless sailor out of the surf. Lifting the two mariners, they carried them through the deep drifts to the fog signal station.

The frozen clothing of the two victims was cut off their bodies, and cold water rubbed on their limbs. Forcing open the seamen's jaws, the rescuers poured stimulants down the throats of the victims. Dry flannels were put on the men. The sailors gradually regained their senses and were given hot food and drink. Soon they were able to tell their story. When they mentioned how their captain had been swept overboard, Hanna learned for the first time of a third man aboard the schooner. The captain's body later washed up on the shore near the scene of the disaster.

The snowstorm was so severe that it was impossible to move the men from the fog signal station until the next day, when they were placed on a bobsled and taken to Hanna's residence. Two days later, as soon as roads were broken through from Portland, the survivors were taken to the city.

In the 1926 Captain Joseph H. Upton succeeded Keeper Frank L. Cotton at Cape Elizabeth Lights. He had served briefly at Matinicus Rock and Cape Elizabeth as assistant keeper before becoming head keeper at the Isles of Shoals in 1913. Born at Cape Elizabeth in 1869, he came back to his home at the age of fifty-seven to become the keeper at Cape Elizabeth Lights.

Late one night in 1934 Captain Upton's wife awoke to find that her husband had not returned from the tower, where he had gone several hours before to adjust the lighting apparatus. Dressing hurridly, she ran out to the tower, where she found him lying unconscious at the foot of the stairs leading up into the turret. He was taken to a Portland hospital and died within a few hours of a double fracture of the skull.

When it was announced in the 1920's that the light in the west tower of Cape Elizabeth was to be dismantled, many mariners protested the act. Since the government, however, had already conducted exhaustive tests before the announcement, it carried out its plans. The light in the west tower has been discontinued for good, it is now believed. The east tower was made into a stronger beacon than any other New England light except Cape Cod. The light now shines from a height of 129 feet above the sea. In World War II it was darkened, but in the summer of 1945 it was relighted.

E. D. Elliot was the keeper in 1937. We visited him several times in his home overlooking the sea and found his cheering smile and pleasant manner typical of the greeting one usually receives from these brave watchmen of the deep.

Most of the lighthouse property has passed into private

hands, but the lower light still stands, looking not radically different from the days of yesteryear.

At the present time Cape Elizabeth Light shines out with a candlepower of 4,000,000. Captain Robert A. Lee, who lives just a few feet away from the light tower with his charming wife and family, tells me that the quarters of the coast guard lifesaving station have been converted to a two-family dwelling where two coast guard officers have their homes.

Gary Merrill of Hollywood purchased the upper light after it was made obsolete. He is seen occasionally during the summer season at his quarters in the western tower.

3

Halfway Rock Light

One of the special locations on the outer rim of Casco Bay is the tiny tower of Halfway Rock. Whether one sees it from the Casco Bay ferry or looks down from an airplane thousands of feet in the air, it gives the feeling of complete isolation. It is a ledge of tragedy, for many a schooner and ship have ended their career at this far-flung beacon.

Located about nine miles out to sea from the center of Portland, deep in Casco Bay, is a pinnacled, jagged ledge from which Halfway Rock Light dominates the entire area. In storms and rough seas the waves sweep entirely over the ledges that extend for several hundred yards to the north and south of the light.

Agitation for a lighthouse at Halfway Rock began more than a century ago when First Lieutenant Green Walden wrote a letter to Captain Joseph Smith, who was inspecting lighthouses and possible sites in the district. Walden said that a light proposed for Mark Island in Casco Bay would be worse than useless, as it would confuse navigators. "I would beg leave to suggest the propriety of erecting a monument on

Halfway Rock," Walden concluded.

Captain Smith concurred in Walden's belief, but thirty years passed and no lighthouse was erected at Halfway Rock. In 1869 fifty thousand dollars was appropriated and construction began at once. The tower was almost finished in 1870 when work stopped for lack of funds. The following year an additional appropriation allowed the light to be completed, and it was illuminated for the first time on August 15, 1871. The light was seventy-six feet above the sea.

The first keeper of Halfway Rock was Captain John T. Sterling, a relative of Robert Thayer Sterling, who was the writer—light keeper. Captain Sterling was justly proud of his attractive station in Casco Bay, and had many visitors during the summer months.

Halfway Rock Light has an unusual system of flashing. According to the recent *Light List* volume, it is "fixed white, alternating with fixed red light, with five sec. red flash in red period, every 90 sec."

The normal white light is 18,000 candlepower, the red flash is of 800,000 strength, and the red light has a beam of 190,000. Changes at the station are planned in the future.

In her delightful book *All Among the Lighthouses*, Mary B. Crowninshield mentions a visit ashore at Halfway Rock in 1885. The lighthouse inspector invited the children of his sister and another young friend to make the regular lighthouse tour with him on the lighthouse tender *Iris*. We read of their visit to Halfway Rock Light:

"The bow oarsman tossed and cleverly boated his oar; then, seizing the painter, dexterously jumped ashore, and, with the assistance of the keepers, who had come down to meet the inspector, hauled the boat well up on the ways, and held her steady until the party were out of her; and then they all walked up to the lighthouse together, the keepers looking fine in their uniforms. 'Such an improvement,' Violet had told the boys, 'over the old way, when they wore anything they happened to have on hand,'—the blue cloth suit with gilt ornaments and buttons giving them a fine and dignified appearance.

" 'That's a queer thing,' said the observing John, as they neared the tower, 'looks like an Esquimau's hut.'

" 'Yes,' answered Uncle Tom. "That was built for a boat-house,—a sort of concrete affair; but you see how little room there is here, and as we had to have another set of boat-ways, it had to be sacrificed.'

"The boys followed Uncle Tom into a circular room at the base of the tower, which seemed to them a sort of storeroom. . . . Uncle Tom's sea-boots were vanishing at the top of the narrow circular iron stairway, and John and Cortland quickly followed. The first room entered was the kitchen of the establishment. There, everything looked in the best possible order, with its neat pantry, finely polished cooking-stove, and shining utensils. The next flight of stairs brought them to another room, the bedroom of the principal keeper; and above this was a second room, with two beds for the assistant keepers. A fourth flight of stairs brought them out in the watch-room, where the keeper remains on duty all night, to see that the light does not go out, and to keep guard generally. . . .

"The keeper opened a door in the lens. . . . The inspector assured himself that the lamp was well cared for, and in good working order,—indeed he asked the opinion on this point of a young man who had come ashore. . . . This young man seemed to speak as one having authority, and the boys found that Uncle Tom spoke of him to the keeper as the 'lampist,' and to him as Mr. Shafer; and that the lampist, though he spoke English but indifferently, seemed to be at home in all matters pertaining to the lamp.

" 'Wind that clock, Hank,' called down the keeper to his assistant in the watch-room below. 'Click, click, click, click,' went the clock. And now a queer frame-work, made of bronze, and set at intervals with perpendicular prisms, outside of which were red panes of glass, began to revolve slowly around the lens proper, and even Cortland could understand, that when it so revolved, the light from the lens could only show forth during the interval, or when there was no red glass to color the light; but, that whenever the colored pane of glass passed any given point, from that point a red beam must shine out across the water."

On September 13, 1966, my wife, Anna-Myrle, and I, together with our daughter Dorothy and my brother Win, went ashore at Halfway Rock from the motorboat *Subojoy*. Head Keeper Horace A. Leverett and Assistant Keepers Robert Shillace and Edward Hannula greeted us. We toured the lighthouse, and Keeper Leverett explained how the foghorn worked.

Severe damage was suffered in the terrible gale of February 18, 1972, when the fuel tank for the generator was washed off the island so that there was no electricity for heat or power for the light for some time. The wood walkway and part of the boat ramp were destroyed. The crew was taken off by helicopter.

4

Forts and Garrisons
of Casco Bay

It is probable that the first fort in Maine was St. George's, built by the Popham colonists at Phippsburg in 1607 at the mouth of the Kennebec River.

Casco Bay Fort was built on the eastern side of the Presumpscot Basin. The fort as well as the settlement at Casco Neck, which later became Portland, were destroyed by the Indians in 1690. Eight years later, because of a treaty, a fort and a trading post for the Indians were erected here. It was here in 1703 that Governor Dudley held his conference with the Indians, who arrived gaily painted and in their native costumes, with several red men from almost every tribe in Maine.

In the next attack, New Casco was the central defense area of all Casco Bay. Five hundred French and Indians attacked the fort, and it was saved only by the arrival of the *Province Galley*, whose guns quickly scattered the fleet of 250 canoes.

Two centuries later, in the year 1924, Governor Percival Proctor Baxter placed in the Maine State Library a wonderful collection of maps that his father, James Phinney Baxter, had compiled. Included was a plan of Casco Bay Fort, built on the Presumpscot River.

The plan identifies the old fort and gives details of the new fort, built around 1698. It was an "oblong square" 250 feet in length and 190 feet in breadth, but the bastions were not included. The covered way was 230 feet in length and ran down to the shore where there was a blockhouse. There is no mark or mention of a palisade enclosure, but the drawings indicate all exterior walls were of timber.

In 1704 Colonel Church recommended that the fort be abandoned, and the House of Representatives ordered it destroyed in 1716. The foundations of New Casco Bay Fort can still be seen and the well can also be identified.

Garrison houses found in most towns differed in construction. Several were ordinary houses converted into garrison houses, to provide a vantage point from which guards could see in every direction. They were constructed for the most part with heavy timbers at least five inches thick, dovetailed at the corners in the manner of a fort. Two stories high, the houses had the upper story projecting above the lower, with the projections often placed on each corner of the upper story so that they could be used as sentry boxes.

A typical structure would be built on a river or harbor facing the direction from which Indian canoes were expected to come. On each corner was a so-called flanker that projected out so that the watchman or sentry inside could see in two directions. On the front of the garrison house a large flanker was usually erected six feet above the entrance so that one could pass directly under it. There were usually three gates, one at each end and one on the side of the front flanker.

The only garrison house still standing today is believed to be the McIntire house in York. Built in 1645, it was enlarged in 1867 and fully restored in 1909 by John R. McIntire.

Every known fort in the general Casco Bay area is included in the following list below, arranged alphabetically.

Alger. Built around 1690, in the Scarboro region.

Allen. Of 1776 vintage, in Falmouth. Named in honor of Colonel Ethan Allen. It was situated on the hill, now the Eastern Promenade.

Anawagon. Prior to 1700, at Southport's Cape Newagen. Mentioned in the New York Colonial Records as one of the Maine defenses against the Indians.

Arrowsic, or Fort Menaskoux. The scene of a conference in 1720 between Indians and soldiers and settlers.

Black Point. Built about 1681 at Scarboro. Largest and strongest fortification ever constructed in the town, although the site was not so favorable for defense as was the location of the Prout's Neck garrison. One hundred acres of land was given by Captain Scottow for the site of the fortification.

Brunswick Fortifications. The earliest defenses, other than Fort George, were probably erected in 1716 by the Pejepscot proprietors, at Small Point and Maquoit. Other garrison houses in or near Brunswick were Dunning, Giveen, Hinkley, Ham's, McFarland's, Minot's, Skolfield's, Burnet Point, and Spear.

Burrows. Constructed in 1813 at Jordan's Point, Portland. Named in honor of Captain William Burrows, who was killed aboard the brig *Enterprise.*

Clark and Lake's. Built about 1658 at Arrowsic's Squirrel Point. Constructed by Thomas Clark and Thomas Lake, who purchased Arrowsic Island from the Indians in 1658.

Foxwell's. Put up about 1750 in Scarboro at Blue Point.

Gorges. Started in 1858 at Hog Island, Portland Harbor. Named for Sir Ferdinando Gorges. A stone fort in a commanding position on a reef, it guarded the entrances to the upper harbor as well as to the ship channel. It was completed about 1864. Although the structure was designed to receive 195 guns, it was found that they were of short range, and heavy ordnance was put in.

Hammond's. Built in 1630 at Woolwich. The site of this fort or garrison house is not exactly known, but it was probably on the northeastern end of Arrowsic Island. The sacking of the fort in 1676 was the initial blow in the eastern part of the state in King Philip's War.

Harpswell Fortifications. They included blockhouses on Bailey Island, on Orr's Island, and on the Neck, all for defense against the Indians. In 1812 an earthwork fort with log foundations was erected at the mouth of the New Meadows River.

Indian Fort. Topsham Island. Tradition, credited by Williamson and other early writers, says that there was an important Indian fortification on the ledge at the end of the bridge. Wharton's Treaty with the Indians was ratified here in 1684. It was sometimes known as Fort Pejepscot.

Loyall. Built in 1680 at Falmouth by the Massachusetts government. Surrendered in 1690 to the French, who destroyed it. The site was probably about thirty feet above the level of the later Grand Trunk Railroad Station, on a hill which has since been demolished.

New Casco. Erected in 1698 at Falmouth. It was a combination fort and trading house. Here, in 1703, an important peace conference with the Indians was held, but in two months the whole area was up in arms. New Casco was a center of defense for all the settlements of Casco Bay. Attacked by a strong force of French and Indians, the fort was saved from capture by the arrival of an armed vessel of the province. In 1716 the fort was demolished by order of the Massachusetts government to avoid the expense of maintaining a garrison.

Newton. Constructed in 1680 at the southern end of Arrowsic Island.

Preble. Begun at Cape Elizabeth, Portland, in 1808, it was completed before the War of 1812. Named for Commodore Preble, prominent in New England's Revolutionary navy. Originally it held eleven or twelve guns, but at the time of the Civil War it was greatly enlarged. The early fortress had white-washed brick ramparts facing the channel, but much of the construction work was of heavy timber.

Prout's Neck "Old Fort." Built in 1703, at Prout's Neck, Scarboro. Located on a sandy bank on the western cove. Here a force of eight men gallantly and successfully resisted an attack of French and Indians.

Scammell. Built in 1808, at House Island, Portland Harbor. Named for a Revolutionary officer, Colonel Alexander Scammell, this was never as extensive a fortification as Fort Preble, but it still possesses an almost unbelievably fascinating dungeonlike interior. It was enlarged at the time of the Civil War to house seventy-one pieces.

Scottow's. Built in 1681 at Prout's Neck. This great stockade on the ridge near the sea could shelter all the inhabitants behind an outside ditch.

Sumner. Erected in 1794 at Portland's Munjoy's Hill. Until 1806 it was the only fortified position in all the harbor according to the book *Maine Forts.*

5

Fort Gorges

A canoe trip to Fort Gorges with my older brother Winthrop in 1967 was almost canceled because of unruly seas. When a Portland television station learned that we would be attempting to reach Fort Gorges that day, they sent a crew in a motor craft to sight us and make sure all was well. We never saw the films they took, but our passenger, writer Ben Kennedy of South Portland, did, and found them interesting.

The trip to Fort Gorges ended successfully, and although several letters I received later from television viewers stated that the canoe trip rivaled a white-water Grand Canyon epic, neither Win nor I thought it was especially noteworthy. Our passenger told us that he had another viewpoint.

Landing at Fort Gorges on that occasion, we pulled our canoe high up on the rocky shore and went through the sallyport of the century-old fortification. There we stood, in silent admiration of the relatively small parade ground of the fort, which never fired a cannon to protect Portland, the city for which it was built.

Fort Gorges can be seen from almost every vantage point in

Casco Bay. Located very close to Little Diamond Island, it cannot be mistaken for any other fort in New England, for it apparently rises right out of the water.

As we rested at the fort, I told of my trip to Washington, D.C., several years before. There I found the undated plans for the construction of Fort Gorges listed as a "memoir and countersigned by the great Sylvanus Thayer," whose statue stands on the military parade grounds at West Point.

The three-page summary of the memoir, "descriptive of the Fort projected for Hog Island Ledge, Portland Harbor, Me.," emphasizes the "importance of the occupation of this point to the defense of Portland Harbor," situated as it was at the bottom of the "main channel of entrance."

The memoir stresses the position of the contemplated fort, for the "fire of a battery placed here is directed upon an incoming vessel, from the time she passed the Lighthouse. From the distance of two miles and more, the vessel is exposed to be raked from this position, while she is approaching and engaged with the guns of Forts Preble and Scammell, both of which must be encountered and passed before any reply can be made to the fire from the Ledge. The deep channel to the east of Bang's Island, by Whitehead is also for the most part of its extent subject to the command of Hog Island Ledge."

Continuing to discuss the fort, Thayer's memoir tells us that the "site selected is as near [as] practicable to Forts Preble and Scammell, and to the channel between Peaks (or House) and Little Hog Island. The projected work has two tiers of gun casemates, and a barbette with masonry parapet. The fire on the main channel between Forts Preble and Scammell is in two fronts of eighteen guns each, crossing their fire down this channel. A front of eighteen guns looks down the Whitehead Channel, which is thus, with the aid of the adjacent faces, exposed to the fire of thirty to forty guns. A front of seventeen guns, together with the barbette fire of the gorge,* covers the rear approach from Casco Bay."

The memoir explains that the "scarp has a thickness of seven feet on the battery fronts and five feet elsewhere. The parapet is six feet thick (except over the thin scarps), and is designed to be constructed of large blocks and with great massiveness."

The plans called for seven casemates for magazine and ordnance purposes, with ten rooms on the west front storerooms, bakery and privy. It was planned that the garrison of 500 men be accommodated in the gun rooms, which were to be closed in during the "severe season." Four sets of officers' quarters were to be in the casemates "of the gorge." Ninety-two guns were planned for Fort Gorges.

Started in 1858, the fort covers an area of 1.5 acres and was built from a model that resembled Fort Sumter in Charlestown.

Constructed of granite instead of brick, Fort Gorges was named for Sir Ferdinando Gorges, the early proprietor of Maine. There are many stories about who the real builder of the fort was, and controversies can be started even at this late date. The names of Reuben Smart, Captain Casey, and Captain J. D. Hurtz all have been suggested from time to time.

Colonel Reuben Staples Smart, a construction engineer, is usually called the builder of Fort Gorges. Born in Swanville, he attended Hampden Academy, and after graduation taught school in the winter months. Tradition says that he was already working at Fort Knox on the Penobscot River when he was ordered by the adjutant general to report to Portland, where he is said to have been given the construction job at once. Colonel Smart landed on Hog Island Ledge with the "first load of granite."

Colonel Smart had nine children by his first wife, and their daughter Valerie fell in love with and married John Murch,

---

*Strangely enough, the word *gorge* is similar to the eventual name of the fort, Gorges. A gorge is the space between bastions of a fort.

mason at the fort. As the granite walls rose higher and higher, a cottage was built inside the fort. There, on March 18, 1863, Annie Gorges Murch was born. But the couple's happiness was short-lived, for yellow fever brought death to the father eighteen months later, and Valerie took her daughter to the Swanville residence of the family.

Meanwhile, Colonel Smart, who was also working at Fort Preble on the mainland, decided to build himself a new home. Choosing the head of South Portland's Pickett Street, directly across from the main gate into Fort Preble, he soon had a house-warming party at what became known as Spear Place. Annie spent much of her childhood there.

As is well known, Fort Gorges never became vital in Casco Bay history, but anyone who wanders around the gigantic fortification must be impressed, especially by the enormous cannon atop the fort, a weapon that weighs considerably more than 20,000 pounds!

Through the years I have taken many groups ashore at Fort Gorges and have always been captivated by the awesome potential of might represented by what is now an abandoned citadel in the middle of Casco Bay.

The city of Portland has great plans for the fort, which should result in an action to make this citadel on Hog Island Ledge easily accessible and attractive.

6

House Island and Fort Scammell

I recall my first visit to romantic House Island, now almost a third of a century ago. The island has a fascinating, mysterious atmosphere, and the dungeons of the fort there give the visitor an almost bewitched feeling, creating a spell that is hard to overcome.

After meeting historian Herbert Jones in Portland one day, I became so impressed by his comments on House Island that I determined to visit the fort as soon as I could. A few days later I landed alone by canoe at the location where Fort Scammell has stood since the year 1808.

On my paddle across from the mainland I had decided that I would make a careful exploration of the underground passages about which Jones had spoken. I was also anxious to locate the only grave left. More than forty memorial stones had stood in the tiny cemetery over a century before, but I never did find any indication of the graveyard, not even the single marker I was told remained.

With the help of Herbert Jones I give you the inscription on the now missing marker, which was the only gravestone on the island in 1945:

IN MEMORY OF
WILLIAM HOGART
WHO DIED MAY 9, 1822
HE WAS A BRAVE SOLDIER
AND AN HONEST MAN

Wandering away from the pier where I had pulled the canoe up above the tide, I walked up to the fortress with its series of musketry loopholes in its thick granite walls. I hunted around the fort until I found a musketry embrasure I could squeeze through. It took a few minutes to become accustomed to the darkness inside the fort. Soon I discovered myself at the top of a long flight of stone stairs which faced another equally lengthy series of granite steps directly across the interior. Both flights dropped down into the dungeon below.

Not only did I find the interior thrilling, but the entire dungeon appealed to me in a strangely fascinating way. Descending the stairs, which ended in a subterranean area, I discovered that the fort itself is vastly different from any other in New England I had ever visited. Having explored both Fort Independence and Fort Winthrop in inner Boston Harbor, I had also carefully found my way around Fort Warren, Fort Andrews, Fort Strong, and Fort Standish farther out to sea. I thought that I had seen almost every type of embattlement, but this Casco Bay stronghold is unlike any of them.

I stood on the cellar floor and looked across at the challenging stone steps ascending upward in the other direction. Granite corridor after granite corridor presented itself to me almost everywhere I turned. Soon I realized that I was completely dominated by what in effect seemed to be part of a medieval fortification approaching in design the interior of the walled city of Carcassonne in France, which was in its final stages the work of the great Sebastien Vauban.

Indeed the various chambers, rooms, staircases, and casemates had been designed by military architects who were masters of creating suspense and mystery.

That moment held me absolutely entranced, and I stood there, my thoughts of the island, the early fort, and of Scammell himself. Suddenly the spell was broken by the distant whistle of a craft passing by, awakening me to reality. Then I heard a scrambling noise as a rat scurried across the stone floor to vanish into a drain, making me wonder if it might be a worthy descendant of John Norwood's famous rodents of another generation.

Among other stories, Herbert Jones had told me of the hermit of the island, John Norwood by name, who lived in a shack or hovel on the island years before, nonchalantly dwelling with a swarm of rats which evidently found him a satisfying host. The details of the manner in which this pied piper of Fort Scammell was able to accomplish the rather unusual feat of living with rats are not known, but Herbert Jones assured me there was considerable truth to the entire story.

Climbing the granite stairs across from those I had used to descend into the dungeon, I was soon at the landing on top of the steps where the musketry loopholes faced Portland. Absolutely unprotected, the landing was a potential danger spot, for one false move could have dropped me down into the dungeon below. I twisted myself across to the loophole window, climbed through, and was out in the sunshine again.

Two hours later the visit to Fort Scammell was but a memory. Landing at Custom House Wharf in Portland, I soon strapped the canoe atop my car and started for home.

The fort on House Island was named for Alexander Scammell. When I visited the National Archives at Washington, D.C., in 1946, I found that Massachusetts-born Scammell had a most interesting life story. Early in his career he had attracted attention while teaching school in Plymouth, Massachusetts, when he and several other gay young blades formed a club in the days before the Revolution. Scammell was one of the princi-pals in a discussion concerning Plymouth Rock which ended with the acceptance of the fact that no one ever recorded in 1620 that Plymouth Rock had been the landing place of the Pilgrims, and the actual physical landing on the Rock was doubtful.

Scammell and his associates, who by this time called them-selves the Old Colony Club, decided to focus attention on the Pilgrims. Therefore, on the morning of December 22, 1769, the one hundred and forty-ninth anniversary of the Landing of the Pilgrims, the Old Colony Club fired a cannon and raised a flag at the Rock, then in its original location on the beach.

A banquet was held that same day at the Howland Tavern on top of Cole's Hill, with an elaborate menu.* Scammell him-self recited an original poem, and the occasion proved so suc-cessful that it was planned to celebrate yearly on the same anniversary. The Old Colony Club then adjourned to its own quarters, where "after much frank regurgitation, as was then allowed in the politest company," they decided to visit Plym-outh Rock itself where a volley of small arms was fired in addition to the earlier celebration involving the cannon and the flag-raising.

Less than three months later the Boston Massacre took place, followed in 1773 by the Boston Tea Party, and the local affairs of the Old Colony Club of Plymouth seemed relatively unim-portant.

Nevertheless, early in the morning of December 22, 1774, the "patriots," anxious to "strike some bold stroke," lined up thirty teams of oxen to accomplish the rather formidable task of bodily moving ancient Plymouth Rock across to Town Square, Plymouth. The chains were attached, but when the signal was given to start the oxen, only the upper part of the Rock fol-

---

*Including Indian whortleberry pudding, clams, oysters, codfish, eel, venison, apple pie, cranberry tarts, cheese, "sauguetash," and frost fish.

lowed. Although it had split away from the lower section, they towed the glacial boulder across town to reach Broad Street and then Town Square, where it remained until 1834. It was then moved to Pilgrim Hall. Eventually, in 1880, it was reunited with the lower section on Plymouth Beach.

When the Revolution came, Alexander Scammell enlisted in the army. The battles of Lexington, Concord, and Bunker Hill were fought in 1775, and Scammell participated in many engagements during the following years. Then, at Yorktown, he was mortally wounded, and was later honored by the United States in the naming of Fort Scammell on House Island. An entire book should be written about this gallant officer.

Engineer H. A. S. Dearborn* began the construction of Fort Scammell in the year 1808. Under authorization of the War Department, Dearborn purchased "for twelve hundred dollars —all the southwest part of Howes, alias House Island, containing twelve acres or more or less." On the highest point of this island an octagonal blockhouse of timber was erected, with a porthole and a gun on each side. The upper story, projecting over the lower two or three feet, contained the battery. "On the low upright center timber of the roof was a carved wooden eagle with extended wings."

Fort Scammell's sister fort lies across on the mainland in Casco Bay, Fort Preble. This fort was also named for an officer of the Revolution, naval hero Edward Preble. Fort Scammell was enlarged in time to be ready for the Civil War, its equipment eventually calling for seventy-one firing areas at that time. However, there is not a single cannon on Fort Scammell today.

The noted explorer Christopher Levett came into Casco Bay in the year 1623, three years after the *Mayflower* reached Plymouth. I quote now from Levett's original journal of his visit:

---

*In whose honor a cannon was fired in Boston Harbor at Dearborn Bastion at Castle Island's Fort Independence on March 16, 1975.

And now in its place I come to Quack,* which I have named *Yorke*. At this place there fished divers ships of *Waymouth* this yeare.

It lyeth about two leagues to the East of *Cape Elizabeth*. It is a Bay or Sound betwixt the Maine and certain Ilands which lyeth in the se about one English mile and halfe.

There are foure Ilands which makes one good harbour, there is very good fishing, much fowle and the mayne as good ground as any can desire. There I found one River wherein the Savages say there is much *Salmon* and other good fish. In this Bay, there hath ben taken this year 4 *Sturgions*, by fishermen who drive only for *Herrings*, so that it is likely there may good store taken if there were men fit for that purpose. This River I made bold to call by my owne name Levetts* river, being the first that discovered it. How farre this river is Navigable I cannot tell, I have ben but 6 miles up it, but on both sides is goodly ground.

In the same Bay I found another River,* up which I went about three miles, and found a great fall, of water much bigger than the fall at *London* bridge, at low water; further a boate cannot goe, but above the fall the River runnes smooth againe.

Just at this fall of water the *Sagamore* or King of that place hath a house, where I was one day when there were two *Sagamors* more, their wives and children, in all about 50. and we were but 7. They bid me welcome and gave me such victualls as they had, and I gave them Tobacco and Aqua vitae.

After I had spent a little time with them I departed & gave them a small shot, and they gave me another. And the

*Portland Harbor and Casco Bay.
*Fore River.
*The Presumpscot.

great *Sagamore* of the East country, whom the rest doe acknowledge to be chiefe amongst them, hee gave unto me a Bevers skin, which I thankfully received, and so in great love we parted. On both sides this river there is goodly ground.

From this harbour to *Sagadahock*, which is about 8 or 9 leagues, is all broken Ilands in the Sea, which makes many excellent good Harbours, where a thousand saile of Shipps may ride in safety; the sound going up within the Ilands to the Cape of *Sagadahock*.

In the way betwixt *Yorke* and *Sagadahock* lyeth *Cascoe*, a good harbour, good fishing, good ground, and much fowle. And I am perswaded that from *Cape Elizabeth* to *Sagadahock*, which is about 30 leagues to follow the Maine, is all exceeding commodious for Plantations: and that there may be 20 good Townes well seated, to take the benefit both of the sea, and fresh Rivers.

For *Sagadahock* I need say nothing of it, there hath been heretofore enough said by others, and I feare me too much. But the place is good, there fished this yeare two ships.

The next place I came to was Capemanwagan,* a place where nine ships fished this yeare. But I like it not for a plantation, for I could see little good timber & leese good ground, there I stayed foure nights, in which time, there came many Savages with their wives and children, and some of good accompt amongst them, as *Menawormet*, a Sagamore, *Cogawesco*, the Sagamore of *Casco* and *Quack* now called *Yorke*, *Somerset*, a Sagamore, one that hath ben found very faithful to the English, and hath saved the lives of many of our Nation, some from starving, others from killing.

*Boothbay.

They extended to have ben gone presently, but hearing of my being there, they desired to see me, which I understood by one of the Masters of the Ships who likewise told me that they had some store of Beaver coats and skinnes, and was going to *Pemaquid* to truck with one Mr. *Witheridge*, a Master of a ship of Bastable, and desired me to use meanes that they should not carry them out of the harbour, I wished them to bring all their truck to one Mr. *Cokes* stage, & I would do the best I could to put it away: Some of them did accordingly, and I then sent for the *Sagamores*, who came, and after some complements they told me I must be their cozen, and that Captain *Gorges* was so, (which you may imagine I was not a little proud of, to be adopted cozen to so many great Kings at one instant, but did willingly accept of it) and so passing away a little time very pleasantly, they desired to be gone, whereupon I told them that I understood they had some coates and Beavers skins which I desired to truck for but they were unwilling, and I seemed carelesse of it (as men must doe if they desire anything of them.) But at last *Somerset* swore that there should be none carryed out of the harbour, but his cozen *Levett* should have all, and then they began to offer me some by way of gift, but I would take none but one paire of sleeves from *Cogawesco*, but told them it was not the fashion of English Captaines alwaies to be taking, but sometimes to take and give, and continually to truck was very good. But in fine, we had all except one coate and two skinnes, which they reserved to pay an old debt with, but they, staying all that night, had them stole from them.

In the morning the *Sagamores* came to mee with a grievous complaint, I used the best language I could to give them content, and went with them to some Stages which they most suspected, and searched both Cabins and Chests, but found noe. They seeing my willingnesse to finde the theefe out, gave mee thankes, and wished me to forbeare saying the Rogues had carried them into the woods where I could not find them.

When they were ready to depart they asked mee where I meant to settle my plantation. I told them I had seene many places to the west, and intended to go farther to the east before I could resolve, they sayed there was no good place, and I heard that *Pemoquid* and *Capmanwagan*, and *Monhiggon* were granted to others, & the best time for fishing was then at hand, which made me the more willing to retire, and the rather because *Cogawesco*, the *Sagamore* of *Casco* and *Quacke*, told me if that I would sit downe at either of those two places, I should be very welcome, and that he and his wife would goe along with me in my boate to see them, which courtesy I had no reason to refuse, because I had set up my resolution before to settle my plantation at *Quacke*, which I named *Yorke*, and was glad of this opportunity, that I had obtained the consent of them who as I conceive hath a natural right of inheritance, as they are the sons of Noah, and therefore doe thinke it fit to carry things very fairly without compulsion, (if it be possible) for avoyding of treacherie.

The next day the winde came faire, and I sayled to *Quacke* or *Yorke*, with the King, Queene, and Prince, bowe and arrowes, dogge and kettell in my boate, his noble attendance rowing by us in their Cannow.

When we came to *Yorke* the Masters of the Shippes came to bid me welcome, and asked what Savages those were, I told them, and I thanked them. They used them kindly, & gave them meate, drinks and tobacco. The woman or reputed Queene, asked me if those men were my friends, I told her they were: then she dranke to them, and told them, they were welcome to her Countrey, and so should all my friends be at any time, she dranke also to her husband, and bid him welcome to her Countrey too, for you must understand that her father was the *Sagamore* of this place, and left it to her at his death having no more Children.

And thus after many dangers, much labour and great charge, I have obtained a place of habitation in *New England*, where I have built a house, and fortified it in a reasonable good fashion, strong enough against such enemies as are those Savage people.

Down through the years many historians have chosen other islands than House for the location of the "house" which explorer Christopher Levett built. After years of research, historian James Phinney Baxter decided that House Island was the only location Levett could have used to construct his edifice. Since that canoe trip, now quite a few years ago, I have gone ashore at House Island on many occasions. Fort Scammell today is said to be the only island fortification in the New World owned by a woman. She is Hilda Dudley, and we have often enjoyed visiting the island to participate in one of the excellent shore repasts she provides. Her party boat, the *Buccaneer*, is well known in Casco Bay.

PART TWO

Battles, Shipwrecks, and the Great Fire

1

Falmouth and the Revolution

Most readers, I am sure, do not realize that when Portland was known as Falmouth, from the earliest days until 1786, the town went through times that were just as difficult to endure as those the areas around Massachusetts experienced. People on many of the peninsulas and islands around Casco Bay actually suffered far more from the red man than the Greater Boston area ever did.

Then when the Revolution came to Maine, the results were in turn far more devastating to the people during the bombardment and burning of Falmouth than in Boston during Bunker Hill and later in the Evacuation, although the history books record the Massachusetts battles in more detail than those in Maine.

Although there were many minor incidents, the real trouble between the Patriots and the Tories in what is now Portland began when Captain Thomas Coulson, a prominent Tory and Falmouth businessman, needed help. He asked for and received the aid of Captain Henry Mowatt, of the British sloop-of-war *Canceau*, to rig his own newly built craft so that he could sail with Captain Mowatt in May of 1775.

Captain Coulson was a Tory, or Royalist, who had run into trouble when he attempted to land some rigging, sails, and stores. Although the supplies were necessary to finish his ship, which was then being constructed at the foot of Falmouth's King Street, the Committee of Inspection had refused to allow him to bring anything ashore and ordered all the goods sent back to England.

Captain Henry Mowatt stepped into the picture and gave Coulson help in outfitting the new craft so that Coulson actually did sail in company with Mowatt during the month of May.

On April 21, 1775, at the height of the controversy between Coulson and the Patriots of Falmouth, news reached Maine of the Battles of Lexington and Concord. Two days later a special town meeting took place, at which time the selectmen were authorized to purchase enough powder to supply the American cannon to defend Falmouth. The Falmouth Minute Men on the Neck were told to turn out four days a week at six pence each a day for training and guard duty. Those living off the Neck were instructed to report three times a week for eight pence a day. It was agreed that if any Minute Man had to march out of the county, he would receive a bounty of twenty-four shillings.

All of this activity took place while the British warship *Canceau*, under Captain Mowatt's watchful eye, was ready to start trouble on her own.

The very day after the town meeting two other British craft came into Casco Bay, after which many residents of Falmouth, fearing trouble, began moving their property out of town. Reverend Thomas Smith states in his journal on April 25, 1775, that "we sent away to Windham our principal things. Our people are many of them doing the same."

On May 7, Colonel Samuel Thompson of Brunswick arrived in Casco Bay with fifty men, planning to destroy Mowatt's *Canceau*. Thompson was not only a lieutenant colonel of the

Brunswick regiment, but a member of the Provincial Congress. Taking his men into a thick grove of pine trees located on the northern side of Munjoy's Hill, he had a view looking down on Sandy Point.

Most people knew nothing of the arrival of the Brunswick group until an event that had far-reaching repercussions took place. It was the capture of Captain Mowatt himself!

The incident occurred when Captain Henry Mowatt, his surgeon, and the Reverend Mr. John Wiswell, a local Tory preacher, were strolling on Munjoy's Hill. The Brunswick colonel noticed Mowatt and captured him along with preacher Wiswell. Indeed, Thompson had a tiger by the tail, and when the local inhabitants discovered what had happened, there was a mixture of jubilation and consternation in the town.

Within an hour the facts became known aboard the *Canceau*, and the officer of the day notified the townspeople that he would lay the town in ashes unless the prisoners were released. Thompson gave an outright refusal. Colonel Phinney, a patriot of Gorham, sent off for his own regiment, while Thompson marched his prisoners down from Munjoy's Hill into Marston's Tavern.

"I thank Providence for throwing Mowatt into my hands," stated Thompson, "and as it is open war between us, it is my duty and policy to retain my prisoners."

Gradually, however, as time went by, more and more citizens visited Colonel Thompson, appealing to him for the release of the British commander. After Captain Henry Mowatt made a personal plea, pledging on his honor as an English gentleman to return without fail the next day, Thompson relented.

We should realize that as Falmouth was then desperately short of provisions and as several supply ships were expected in port, there was a strong group of Falmouth residents in favor of letting Mowatt go aboard the *Canceau* if only for a few hours to save face. Under a flag of truce, supervised by General Jedediah Preble and Colonel Freeman, the captain returned to his ship. Mowatt still swore on his word as "an English gentleman" that he would return ashore in Falmouth as agreed.

By morning more troops poured into Falmouth, six hundred strong, and when their officers heard that Mowatt had been allowed to return to his ship, they were so enraged that they ordered the house arrest of both Preble and Freeman, and refused them food! The two men were released later on condition that they would furnish refreshment to the visiting militia.

Colonel Thompson proved to be right in his desire to keep his prisoner, for Mowatt violated his parole and did not return to Falmouth. Essentially the town was now under military law, but it was an edict that in actuality tolerated lawlessness for the soldiers themselves. Not being under proper supervision, the enlisted men went to Captain Coulson's home and rifled it, after which they turned the building into a veritable barracks. Homes of other well-known Tories were also robbed.

A soldier named Calvin Lombard, inspired by the liquor found in Coulson's cellar, loaded his musket and went down to the waterfront on King Street. There he aimed at the *Canceau* a short distance offshore and fired two shots, each of which penetrated deep into the warship's hull!

A group then seized Coulson's boat on the shore and the next day pulled and pushed it through the streets and fields to a point where the Third Parish Church stood two generations later. Another British boat was hauled to the same location the following morning.

"Gentleman" Mowatt now ordered that Calvin Lombard be surrendered because of his act of violence, demanding that the "mob from the country" be dispelled and the boats restored, or he would open fire on the town. Lombard was not surrendered, but slowly the out-of-town troops returned to their homes, the last of them leaving on May 13.

Mowatt still felt uneasy, having heard that cannon were to be brought into Falmouth, cannon that could easily be trained on the *Canceau*. But when all outside troops left and many of the people assured Mowatt that they disapproved of the "armed body," Mowatt and Coulson sailed away, and the people of Casco Bay were able to breathe more easily.

On June 7, 1775, the British warship *Senegal*, of sixteen guns and with two tenders, arrived in Casco Bay, followed five days later by Captain Coulson in his new ship. Coulson planned to take aboard a cargo of masts and spars. This called for action by the Patriots of Maine, who moved the masts and timbers up the river beyond his reach. With Coulson came Tory Sheriff Tyng. The townspeople allowed the two men to invite their wives aboard but refused Coulson, "a declared enemy of the country," permission to put his cargo on the craft, for there was a resolve of Congress to that effect regarding enemies.

On June 22, one of Coulson's boats that had gone up the Presumpscot River in an effort to load masts and spars was seized along with five men and three guns. The men were released but the property was kept. Coulson then sailed away, his plans thwarted.

On October 16, 1775, Captain Henry Mowatt again sailed into Casco Bay aboard the *Canceau*, accompanied by another warship, the *Cat*, two schooners and a bomb sloop. The apprehensive citizens hoped that Mowatt was merely on a trip for hay and cattle, and the authorities dispatched two companies of soldiers to two nearby islands to prevent Mowatt's men from taking over the area near the anchored *Canceau*. The five British craft were then warped up the harbor to form a barrier "fronting the principal settlements on the Neck."

The seriousness of Mowatt's visit was conveyed in a letter the captain sent ashore on October 17, in which he stated that he was in Casco Bay to carry out "a just punishment." He gave them only two hours to remove themselves from the scene of danger!

The officer who landed with this terrible message came ashore at the lower end of India Street and walked through a "prodigious assembly of people" on his way to the Town House.

The letter was delivered to lawyer Theophilus Bradbury, later Supreme Court Justice of Massachusetts, who read the awesome statement to the people. The letter follows:

After so many premeditated attacks on the legal prerogative of the best of sovereigns, after the repeated instances you have experienced in Britain's long forbearance of the rod of correction, and the manifest and paternal extension of her hands to embrace again and again, have been regarded as vain, and nugatory; and in place of a dutiful and grateful return to your King and parent State, you have been guilty of the most unpardonable rebellion, supported by the ambition of a set of designing men, whose insidious views have cruelly imposed on the credulity of their fellow creatures, and at last have brought the whole into the same dilemma, which leads me to feel, not a little, the woes of the innocent of them in particular on the present occasion, from my having it in orders to execute a just punishment on the town of Falmouth, in the name of which authority I previously warn you to remove without delay, the human specie out of the said town, for which purpose I give you the time of two hours, at the period of which, a red pennant will be hoisted at the main top gallant mast head, with a gun. But should your imprudence lead you to show the least resistance, you will in that case, free me of that humanity so strongly pointed out in my orders as well as in my inclination.

I do also observe, that all those who did on a former occasion fly to the king's ship under my command, for protection, that the same door is now open to receive them.

The officer who will deliver this letter, I expect to return immediately unmolested.

I am, & c.,

H. Mowatt.

After the reading of this astounding declaration, a frightful consternation gripped the assembly, and there was a silence that lasted for several moments. Desperate, the populace quickly chose Brigadier Preble, Dr. Nathaniel Coffin, and a lumber merchant from Scotland, Robert Pagan, as a committee to wait on Captain Mowatt aboard the *Canceau.*

The British ships had sailed directly to Falmouth from Boston with orders from Admiral Graves to carry out the destruction of the town at once. The three men appointed to visit Captain Mowatt received no attention at first, being ignored, but eventually Mowatt informed them of the admiral's orders and said that the townspeople would have until eight the following morning to get out of town, providing that small arms were turned over to the British with all ammunition.

After going ashore, the three delegates informed the populace what the terms were. Of course the townspeople "disapproved of the terms," but in order to gain time to remove the women and children, the sick, and what property could be moved, they sent out eight small arms that very night.

Returning to the *Canceau* early the next morning, the committee of three hoped to get a little additional time. Unfortunately for them, at eight thirty Mowatt requested them to go ashore, telling the three that he would start firing the cannon within half an hour.

Promptly at nine that morning, October 17, 1775, Captain Henry Mowatt ordered the red flag hoisted to the top of the mast, and the guns began firing!

A constant cannonading of shells, musket balls, grapeshot, and three- to nine-pound cannonballs began to rain down on the defenseless town of Falmouth. Captain Mowatt now introduced his most diabolical tactic, known as firing the carcass bombs. He ordered the howitzers and mortars to be loaded with carcass shells, which were actually hollow shells filled with combustibles especially chosen to set fire when landing on houses and other buildings ashore.

As if this were not enough, Mowatt sent special parties ashore from the British ships with fire bombs. The first house set afire was that of Mr. Bailey, which was located at the corner of Middle Street where Federal Street joined it.

In all, more than one hundred British sailors landed from the fleet, and confusion in the streets was overwhelming. No plan of defense against the enemy had been thought of, and none was carried out. The American soldiers, who returned from the Casco Bay Islands that morning, were so busy helping families carry out their goods that they offered no resistance.

Although no resident of Falmouth was killed, one Reuben Clough, residing at the corner of Plum and Fore Street, was seriously wounded. Several British marines were killed and quite a number wounded in placing and firing powder charges to destroy strategic buildings.

The fire gained terrible headway, and it was not long before a solid "broad sheet of flame" had spread rapidly through the various areas of Falmouth. Every house was destroyed from Jordan's Point to Exchange Street as far as School Street with the exception of the residences of Sheriff Tyng and Theophilus Bradbury on the corner of Willow Street. All homes in India Street and Turkey Lane were gutted. In all 136 dwellings were destroyed. With them went the Episcopalian Church, the Court House, the Town House and the Custom House, a new fire engine, and almost all the stores and warehouses in town.

Not more than half of the movables were saved from the burning buildings, with more than 160 families turned out of doors. The last home to suffer destruction was that of the Reverend Mr. Smith. It caught fire from the blaze in the Captain Sanford residence, which was on the northwest corner of India Street.

On the waterfront every wharf except two short ones and every craft except two that the enemy sailed away were burned and destroyed. Several marines attempted to set fire to the First Parish Meeting House but were stopped.*

Nor was this all, for deserters from the fleet told the residents that the British intended to take possession of the Neck and improve the Casco Bay area so that ships of the British fleet could use the harbor for the winter.

Extreme hardships to the inhabitants resulted, of course, and on November 10 the Provincial Congress granted two hundred and fifty pounds to the sufferers and offered fifteen bushels of corn sent to any family whose loss prevented them from obtaining the corn in the usual way.

Then came another scare, the arrival of the ship *Cerebus*, whose commander, John Symons, issued orders forbidding the inhabitants from fortifying Munjoy's Hill. Nevertheless, the residents went right ahead and erected breastworks and batteries against the enemy there. Working all day Sunday, they constructed a battery in which they placed both their available cannon, six-pounders. Many volunteers, hearing of the arrival of the *Cerebus* at Falmouth Harbor, crowded into town. But the *Cerebus* and Commander Symons sailed away without making an issue of the Munjoy's Hill fortifications.

Incidentally, on November 2, 1775, Enoch Moody wrote to General George Washington that when the *Cerebus* arrived with four hundred sailors and marines, there were only two half-barrels of powder in all the town, not really enough to provide any sort of opposition. He told General Washington that the entire area needed a person of "martial spirit."

During the last month of 1775 a committee was chosen to join other Maine towns in the vicinity to consider measures for the safety of Cumberland County. On May 21, 1776, two forts, one on Munjoy's Hill and the other on the Free Street Hill, were

---

*The First Parish Meeting House remained standing for more than half a century, after which it was torn down. In the process of demolition in 1826, the building was found to contain several cannon balls and quite a little grape shot.

chosen for repairs. A few weeks later the General Court sent ten cannon to Falmouth and made provision for fifty soldiers to be stationed in the town.

Actually, after the 1775 trouble, Falmouth itself was not subjected to attack by British warships, and gradually Casco Bay became a rendezvous for Revolutionary privateers. Falmouth was the location of shipyards which built many of these privateers.

The experience that one of these privateers, the *Retrieve*, met was not successful. Fitted with ten guns, she was captured at sea and ended her privateering career in Halifax.

Another craft, the *Fox*, was armed with four guns and scythes to be used as swords. When only eight days out, the *Fox* came up alongside an eighteen-gun craft with a valuable cargo, which she captured and brought into Boston. Although her master on this first trip was not identified, a Captain Stone was her commander in later cruises.

In 1778 the brig *Union* was fitted out with twelve guns, but six were merely painted wooden models.

In April, 1777, Abner Lowell was put in charge of eighty men stationed at the Neck, and also was in command of another forty men at Cape Elizabeth.

Strangely enough, when Burgoyne was captured, the celebration at Falmouth brought the death of twenty-eight-year-old Ben Tukey, killed when a gun exploded prematurely.

When in 1778 a resolve was passed to recruit two thousand men, Falmouth was especially mentioned as being "highly commendable, manly and patriotic in their glorious exertions to raise volunteers."

During that year of 1778 the dreaded smallpox broke out, with five youths successfully treated for the sickness and forty-one others entering the pest house to await developments. The year was also noted for the complete turnabout in the attitude of the French. France had been a thorn in the flesh of Maine residents for openly helping the Indians early in Falmouth's history. But from this point on France gave both spiritual and practical aid to the cause of the Colonies.

Continental money issued between June 22, 1775, and November, 1779, totaled $241,552,780. Unfortunately, all during this time it was depreciating in value. By October 1, 1781, four dollars in paper was needed to equal one dollar of silver!

Luckily, the season of 1779 brought bountiful harvests, and as William Willis tells us, "saved the country from the horrors of famine." Also commenting on the good harvest, Reverend Thomas Smith wrote in his journal that "never was the corn so forward," and emphasized the news that 1779 was a "wonder of a potatoe year, so many, so large and so good."

On the other side of the ledger, Falmouth heard of the arrival of a British fleet under the command of Captain "Henry Mowat Senr. Officer" at Penobscot Bay. Although the Colonial Government sent 1500 men and a fleet of nineteen vessels, the results were disastrous to the Americans. Poor planning brought the expected victory to dismal defeat. Although George Washington knew nothing of the plans, Dudley Saltonstall and General Solomon Lovell led a total of 2900 Americans to defeat at Bagaduce's Fort George on the Penobscot River. Paul Revere, chief of artillery, did not distinguish himself during this campaign, being court-martialed for cowardice, a charge of which he was later cleared. Saltonstall's efforts were so weak that they ended his career forever.* Every American craft was either sent to the bottom, captured, or burned!

Barely had the disquieting news of the Penobscot Bay debacle been disclosed when, on September 3, three vessels, two of them warships, appeared off Casco Bay, and there were fears that Bagaduce's disaster might be repeated at Casco Bay. Batteries were quickly constructed in three areas, Free Street, India

*There are two sketches of the catastrophe which I possess, one drawn "by an Officer present," and another by John Calef, a Massachusetts Loyalist.

Street, where Fort Loyal had stood, and the brow of Munjoy's Hill.

Actually, the two warships entering Falmouth Harbor were the American frigates *Deane* and *Boston*, not British craft at all. The *Boston*, built at Newburyport and carrying twenty-four guns, had captured many prizes, while the *Deane* had also covered herself with glory.

No further scares affected the residents of the Falmouth area that year of 1779, but in 1780 the British began to strike out again, and when winter came the people of Falmouth heard of General Peleg Wadsworth's defeat at Thomaston. William Willis tells us that "an abandoned traitor" led the British forces to the Wadsworth quarters in February, 1791, and not only was the general wounded but he was captured as well. Taken to Fort George at Bagaduce, he languished in captivity until escaping the following June, reaching Falmouth within a few days.

Incidentally, Reverend Smith, famous for his *Journal*, on May 8, 1781, made his slave Romeo a free man, and recorded the event with the following statement: "I liberate and give up all right, claim, and title to him and his service, and to all intents and purposes to be his own or a *Free man.*" Romeo had fought for three years for the Continental forces.

On March 31, 1783, news reached Falmouth that the war was truly over, and on April 4 a handbill was issued in town confirming the news. Smith states in his *Journal* that the town "had a mad day of rejoicing, firing cannon incessantly from morning to night among the houses, and ended in killing Mr. Rollins." Samuel Rollins met his death when of one of the cannon fired during the celebration burst.

The definitive treaty, as Willis tells us, was signed September 3, 1783, thus ending the Revolutionary War.

2

The *Boxer* and the *Enterprise*

One day the Portland poet Henry Wadsworth Longfellow took a walk around Munjoy's Hill and down to a waterfront fortification.

"I lay down," he related, "in one of the embrasures and listened to the lashing, lulling sound of the sea just at my feet. It was a beautiful afternoon, and the harbor was full of white sails, coming and departing."

Longfellow mentions that he wrote a poem, "a memory of Portland,—my native town, the city by the sea." I quote that part of Longfellow's poem relating to the battle that is the subject of this chapter:

> Often I think of the beautiful town
> That is seated by the sea;
> Often in thought go up and down
> The pleasant streets of that dear old town
> And my youth comes back to me.
>
> . . .
>
> I remember the sea-fight far away
> How it thundered o'er the tide!

And the dead captains, as they lay
In their graves, o'erlooking the tranquil bay
Where they in battle died.
And the sound of that mournful song
Goes through me with a thrill:
"A boy's will is the wind's will,
And the thoughts of youth are long, long thoughts."

In the Eastern Cemetery of Portland's Munjoy's Hill, buried side by side, lie Lieutenant William Burrows, Captain Samuel Blythe, and Midshipman Kervin Waters, all participants in the sea battle mentioned by Longfellow. The encounter between the British brig *Boxer* and the American brig *Enterprise* took place during the War of 1812 off the coast of Maine.

Although the *Constitution* has been called the luckiest American fighting ship, I think that we should also consider the career of the *Enterprise*. Of all the vessels that have sailed the seven seas, even the *Constitution* did not have as many lucky victories as the *Enterprise*.

Launched in 1800 and rigged as a schooner, the *Enterprise* was armed with twelve six-pounders. She was sent to the West Indies to attack French privateers and soon took eight of these craft, including the proud *Flambeau*, which carried 110 men in her crew as compared with the *Enterprise*'s complement of 83.

A year later the *Enterprise* crossed to the Mediterranean, where she overcame the pirate craft *Tripoli*, which carried 14 guns and 80 men. The pirate vessel surrendered after 20 of her men were killed and 30 wounded. The *Enterprise* did not lose a man.

The *Enterprise* now captured the ketch *Mastico*, which was later rechristened the *Intrepid*.* Rerigged as a brig, the *Enter-*

---

*The immortal Stephen Decatur sailed into Tripoli Harbor aboard the *Intrepid* in 1804 to burn the *Philadelphia* so she could not be taken over by the enemy, but the *Intrepid* blew up in the encounter.

prise was commissioned as a coast guard vessel to cruise between Cape Ann and the Bay of Fundy. First she was captained by Master Commandant Johnston Blakeley. By the Act of January 2, 1813, Blakely was appointed master of the ill-fated sloop-of-war *Wasp*,* and Lieutenant William Burrows took command of the *Enterprise.*

On September 4, 1813, the *Enterprise* sailed for Monhegan Island. The very next morning, while off Pemaquid, Lieutenant Burrows sighted a craft that proved to be the British brig *Boxer.*

The crew of the *Enterprise* were more than eager to show the British vessel that they were ready for battle. When the rumor passed around that Burrows was going to run instead of fight, a protest went up. But the men were wrong, for the *Enterprise* was merely maneuvering for position.

At three o'clock that afternoon the topmen ran aloft to furl the lighter sails. The braces were manned, and the two craft steadily approached each other. When within "a half pistol shot," both brigs cut loose with broadsides.

Several of the *Enterprise* crew manning one of the quarterdeck guns were struck by enemy fire. As was often the custom, they all cheered as they fired and were just beginning to reload when the enemy shot killed them.

The survivors, now shorthanded, found themselves hard-pressed. Burrows saw that his men needed help and decided to join the group who were trying to haul out the guns for the next round. Running to their aid, the captain grasped the tackle fall with both hands, braced his foot against the port sill, and put his weight on the tackle with the other men.

Suddenly a canister shot from the *Boxer* entered through the gunport, striking Captain Burrows in the upper part of the leg by which he braced himself. The shot then bounced off his thighbone to bury itself in the unfortunate officer's abdomen! In the language of the day it was a "fearful wound." Nevertheless,

*The *Wasp* disappeared mysteriously with Captain Blakeley and all hands aboard and was never heard from again, as I tell in *Fury of the Seas.*

William Burrows refused to be carried below, insisting that "the colors must never be struck."

Lieutenant Edward R. McCall now took command. This was one of the few instances in naval history when a subordinate, forced to take over a warship at the height of battle, did as well as his superior would have done. Cannon fire from the *Enterprise* continued to be just as effective as before. Her rather ordinary sailing ability actually improved and was now definitely superior to that of the enemy.

As the *Enterprise* forged ahead, McCall eased her sheets, hauling down the foresail to run across the bows of the *Boxer*, after which the *Enterprise* raked the British craft again and again with the starboard battery, which up to that point had seen little action.

Standing the fire, those aboard the *Boxer* attempted to return shot for shot until about 3:45 P.M., when the British realized their hopeless situation. An officer appeared high on the topgallant forecastle to shout that, although all the colors had been nailed firmly to the spars, the *Boxer* was surrendering.

A young lieutenant aboard the *Boxer* then created a sensation by shouting out, "No, no, no," adding some "pretty strong words" immediately afterward, but he was subdued by his fellow officers. Men were then sent aloft to tear the British flags down from the spars and bring them to the deck.

The Americans, led by James Poland, newly commissioned as a captain boarded the *Boxer* to discover that Captain Samuel Blythe of the British craft had been mortally wounded early in the engagement. Poland received the traditional sword of surrender and later took it aboard the *Enterprise*, where it was presented to the new commander, Lieutenant McCall. He, however, was reluctant to accept the sword of surrender. Carrying the sword to Captain Burrows, McCall handed it to his superior officer, who grasped the weapon with both hands.

"I am satisfied. I die content," were the final words of Captain Burrows, and he collapsed, dropping Captain Blythe's sword to the deck.*

The two craft had been almost evenly matched. The *Boxer* was a few tons larger in size, and her officers and crew had seen far more action in battle than the Americans. Although the *Enterprise* carried more guns and men, her officers did not have the experience the British had.

Editorially, the London *Times* stated on October 22, 1813, that the "*Boxer* was literally cut to pieces in sails, rigging, spars, and hull; whilst the *Enterprise*" was in condition to be able to start renewed action immediately afterward.

Later the *Boxer* was inspected by Commodore Isaac Hull, captain of the *Constitution*. There will always be doubt as to the exact number in the crew of the *Boxer*, because when Commodore Hull estimated that she had one hundred men on board, he meant only men before the mast and petty officers, and did not include the commissioned officers.

We do know that aboard the *Boxer* thirty-five were killed. The loss on the *Enterprise* were four killed and eight wounded. Eventually the *Boxer* accompanied the victorious *Enterprise* into Portland Harbor, and a memorial service was conducted for the dead. Lieutenant Burrows and Captain Blythe were buried side by side at Munjoy's Hill with the highest honors possible. Interred with the two officers in Eastern Cemetery was Midshipman Kervin Waters of the *Enterprise*.The slab on the grave of Lieutenant Burrows, which is the central tomb of the three, reads as follows:

Beneath this stone moulders the body of Lt. William Burrows, late commander of the United States brig *Enterprise*, who was mortally wounded Sept. 5, 1813 in action which continued to increase the fame of American valor by cap-

*The sword was later presented to a relative, Silas M. Burrows, and passed through generations of descendants. It is now in Marshfield, Massachusetts.

turing His British Majesty's brig *Boxer* after a severe contest of 45 minutes. Age 28 years. A passing stranger has erected this monument out of respect to the name of a patriot who in the hour of peril obeyed the loud summons of an injured country and who gallantly met and conquered the foeman.

On the right of the Burrows tomb is the grave of the British captain, on which the following words are inscribed:

In memory of Capt. Samuel Blythe, late commander of His Britannic Majesty's brig *Boxer*. He nobly fell Sept. 5, 1813 in action with the United States brig *Enterprise*. In death glorious, his country will long deplore one of her bravest sons, his friends long lament one of the best of men. Age 29 years. The surviving officers of his crew offer this feeble tribute of respect and admiration.

A medal was later voted by Congress to the nearest male relative of the dead American captain, Silas M. Burrows of New York, who was the "passing stranger" of the tomb inscription. Another medal was awarded to Edward R. McCall, who took command of the *Enterprise* when his superior officer was mortally wounded.

The next assignment of the *Enterprise* was a trip to Charleston, where she was employed as a harbor guard until the end of the war. The *Enterprise* disappeared from the records a short time later.

A final thought on the *Boxer-Enterprise* contest was suggested by Harrison Brown in 1963 on the 150th anniversary of the battle. There is only one other known location in the New World where a parallel in history exists. In Quebec City a monument stands to General James Wolfe and the Marquis Louis-Joseph Montcalm, the two commanders of the British and French forces on the Plains of Abraham. In 1759 both leaders were killed in the same engagement, which broke French power in America forever. The translation on the Quebec monument tells us that valor gave them a common death, history a common fate, posterity a common monument:

MORTEM VIRTUS COMMUNEM, FAMAM HISTORIA,
MOMENTUM POSTERITAS DEDIT.

3

Read and the *Caleb Cushing*

From what I have been able to discover in forty-three years of research concerning Casco Bay and the entire Maine coast, it is apparent that historians have ignored many important Maine events. These occurrences include Indian battles, piracy, shipwrecks, devastating fires, and outstanding naval battles of both the War of 1812 and the Civil War. Possibly the dramatic life of a young hero of the Confederacy stands at the top of such obvious omissions.

In May, 1863, Second Lieutenant Charles W. Read was detached from the *C. S. Florida* and went aboard the prize brig *Clarence*. His subsequent war career had few moments not crowded with excitement.

Some forty years ago I investigated Read's record with three Civil War enthusiasts* at Fort Warren in Boston Harbor, where Read had twice been a Confederate prisoner almost three quarters of a century before. Later I did additional research at the Maine Historical Society regarding Read's Casco Bay exploits.

*Dr. William Flynn, John G. Weld, and Charles O. Hurd.

Lieutenant Read, an Annapolis graduate and blockade runner, told in his own words how he began his career of burning and sinking Northern craft.

"I received from the *Florida* one howitzer and twenty men, including an engineer. On the twelfth of June, I captured the Yankee bark *Tacony*, and as she was a much better vessel than the *Clarence*, I transferred everything to the former and burned the latter vessel. Between the 12th and the 24th of June I burned or bonded* nineteen sail.

"On the morning of the 25th of June I burned the *Tacony* and transferred everything to the prize schooner *Archer*. On the 26th at sunset I anchored in the harbor of Portland, Me., and at 1:30 the following morning boarded and captured the U.S. Revenue Cutter, *Caleb Cushing*. Day dawned before the cutter could be got out of the range of the forts, and I was in consequence hindered from firing the shipping in the harbor. At eleven A.M., when about 20 miles east of Portland Light, we were attacked by two large steamers and three tugs. After expending all our ammunition I blew up the cutter and surrendered in small boats."

Such is the brief statement of Lieutenant Read, which he wrote at Fort Warren on July 30, 1863.

Let us go back to the October day in 1862 when Charles W. Read was commissioned a second lieutenant in the Confederate Navy.* "Several young incompetents" had been sent to Commander John N. Maffitt aboard the commerce-destroyer *Florida*, who caused Maffitt "to groan within," according to naval historian Winfield M. Thompson. One of them, however, gave promise of being a different sort of sailor than those who had been discouraging Maffitt with their lack of discipline and interest.

*Bonding was an agreement by the master of the captive vessel to pay to the Confederacy at a future date a sum of money equivalent to the value of the cargo and craft taken.
*See the journal of Commander John N. Maffitt, C.S.N.

As Thompson wrote years later, greeting "this young officer, the harassed commander of the *Florida* saw that here he had a subordinate who would one day prove of value to him. 'He is the best they have sent me,' thought Commander Maffitt, as he looked upon the slim, boyish figure and into the thin face and brown eyes of the young officer.

"Though but 23 years old, Lieutenant Read had already earned a place of honor among his brother officers in the Confederate service. Graduated from the Naval Academy in 1860—at the bottom of his class of 25 men, for dreaming and scheming and reading the stories of old sea rovers had pleased him better than the routine of study—Read, in his first year of service afloat, had been compelled, by events, like every other officer in the navy, to make a declaration of his allegiance. Although others of his class, from border states, had cast their lot with the North—Winfield Scott Schley, of Maryland, and John C. Watson, of Kentucky, whose names are now on the list of rear-admirals, were among them—Read, whose home was in Mississippi, never hesitated a moment in surrendering his rank of midshipman as soon as the first gun was fired in the great contest, and enlisting in the naval arm of the Confederate service.

"Read boarded the *Florida* with more than a year of active service to his credit—service that had sent him more than once, on the Mississippi, through a hell of fire—but he had not yet tasted the delights of sea roving. He yearned for an opportunity to prey on merchantmen owned in the North, and secure reprisal, in a measure, for the losses his family had sustained in the path of war in Mississippi. His views of war were in accord with such a method. His ideal of a sailor had always been the free fighter of the glorious old days of sail. More than once he had pored over the romantic adventures of Paul Jones. The struggles and achievements of that heroic adventurer were an inspiration to him. He felt such deeds were not entirely things of the past, and often in his conversations with intimates he had talked of raids against the enemy that should be as full of dash, danger and the possibilities of success as those of Jones in the waters of the British Isles.

"When, therefore, Read stood on the deck of the *Florida*, he felt he had at last arrived at a goal of his ambition. From his commanding officer, and others on board, he heard with a thrill of excitement the story of the *Florida*'s brief but stirring career since her departure as a merchantman from England—of her arrival at Nassau, her arrest and release there; of the man-killing labor of putting aboard her guns and stores in the intense heat of midsummer at Green Cay; of the horrors of yellow fever, with which the crew were stricken as they worked, and the terrible labors of Lieutenant Maffitt, to succor the dying, there being no doctor on board; of the escape to Cardenas, where the ship lay for days helpless off the town, when scarce a man could raise his head.

"In the breast of Read the fire of adventurous ardor was fanned to a clear flame. He was in a fever to get to sea.

"Anxiously all hands watched the weather as the month of December, 1862, dragged along its dismal days, for a dark and stormy night was necessary to escape. But still orders did not arrive for the vessel to sail. In all the ship's company no one was so impatient at the delay as Read. On every dark night, and in every passing squall, he saw an opportunity to get away.

"At last, on the night of the 16th of January, 1863, the nervous tension of all on board reached its height, for orders were given to get the vessel underway, and make for the bar.

"Slipping their cables, the blockaders gave chase. The *Florida*, under all sail and steam, with a half gale to help her, was making 14½ knots when she passed the blockaders, and secured a lead they could not overcome. The chase lasted all day, and at night the Confederate had run all her pursuers hull down but two. Next morning she was alone, with nothing in sight but foaming seas and black flying clouds.

"Thus was her cruise against the shipping of the North begun—a cruise destined to be second only to that of the *Alabama*.

"The young officers of the *Florida* were not long in getting their first taste of adventure at sea. Prizes were taken the following day, and rich prizes, too. All the dreams of Read's youth, all the schemes he had devised for the Confederacy, seemed possible in such a sphere of action as this.

"Read unfolded various plans for further raids on the enemy's shipping, and Lieutenant Maffitt was agreeable. The plan that was nearest his heart, and which most appealed to the *Florida*'s commander, involved the employment by Lieutenant Read of a merchantman prize, to be manned by a picked crew, for the purpose of entering a Northern port and cutting out a fast steamer, and firing shipping in that port."

As he explained later, Commander Maffitt cherished a hope of going to the North himself, in the *Florida*, but he could not see his way clear to abandon his successful Southern cruise, even "to give the coast of New England a small appreciation of war troubles," as he says in his journal. To send a subordinate was then the best thing he could do to further his plan, and Lieutenant Read, he believed, could make such a mission a success if any man could.

The *Florida*'s commander, therefore, agreed to Lieutenant Read's plan, and they waited for a prize suited to their purpose. On the morning of May 6, 1863, a clear, hot day, with a smart trade wind blowing, her lookout sighted a brig to leeward. After a short chase the *Florida* slowed down, showed her colors, and hailed the brig, which proved to be the square-rigger *Clarence*, of Baltimore, from Rio with a cargo of coffee.

Lieutenant Read with a boat's crew boarded the *Clarence*. Her captain lost no time in giving assurances of surrender. He feared being sent to the bottom by the guns he knew were concealed behind the black bulwarks of the steamer rolling easily in the long swell less than half a mile to weather of him. Lieutenant Read examined the brig's papers, found them regular, and then looked over the vessel.

As Thompson stated later, the *Clarence* was about 250 tons burden and stoutly built, though her lines gave more than a hint that her sailing qualities were doubtful. She had little if any shear, and a half ellipitical stern. Her bowsprit was short, she had no royals, and she carried no canvas above the main topmast staysail. The end of her main boom did not extend beyond the taffrail. Her deck arrangement included a house forward of the foremast and an afterhouse, the top of which came just above the rail, and had an iron railing around it. She was painted black, with a white stripe around the bulwarks.

Read's call for volunteers produced more men than he could take. A selection was made from among the most daring in the *Florida*'s crew. Not a man among them was reluctant to face the danger.

As the steamer passed the brig, now filling away on a northerly course, her crew lined the side. Waving their caps, they gave three cheers for the little band on the *Clarence*. The cheers were returned, and the two vessels parted company. In less than an hour the *Florida* was hull down, and Lieutenant Read had time to indulge in some sober thoughts on the enterprise in which he was embarked, and on the requirements of his role as a peaceful merchantman.

The *Clarence*'s new crew found the management of the vessel a source of interest and instruction, for many of them had never been on a square-rigger before. To prepare for their campaign they made a fine battery of Quaker (or false) guns from some spare spars, and painted them to represent the gray muzzles of heavy ordnance. These guns, as well as the brass howitzer brought aboard from the *Florida*, were kept concealed behind the bulwarks to be mounted when needed.

On June 9, in latitude 32° 52' N, longitude 74° 6' W, the brig
Mary Alvina, sailing from Boston to New Orleans with army
stores, was captured and burned. From prisoners and papers
taken from the *Whistling Wind*, which had been captured June
8, and the *Mary Alvina*, Lieutenant Read gleaned information
of a state of affairs at Hampton Roads that would prevent
carrying out his plans to capture a steamer there, for no vessel
was allowed to enter except those with stores for the government. There was a strong guard of gunboats above Fortress
Munroe and sentries on every wharf. Outside the fort were two
boarding steamers. Baltimore also was guarded by gunboats in
the bay. Read was therefore powerless, even in his peacelike
disguise, and some change of plan was necessary. He decided
to cruise into New England waters, where Commander Maffitt
had promised to meet him about June 20, if circumstances
permitted.

The *Clarence*, foul from her long voyage, and at best a slow
craft, was not the proper vessel for such an undertaking. Read
determined to transfer his crew to the first prize better suited
to his work, and so informed his men. Since they were over-
whelmingly tired of the square-rigger, they were eager to make
a change.

On the morning of June 21 the *Clarence*, when forty miles
off Cape Charles—latitude 37° N, longitude 75° 30' W—sighted
a bark also standing north, and overtook her in the light southerly wind. Shortly the *Clarence* luffed, and brought the bark
into the wind with a shot from the howitzer.

Lieutenant Read regarded her well as she backed her topsails
and lay close aboard awaiting a visit from the *Clarence*'s boat.
She was about 400 tons, and in ballast, her copper showing
below the load line, as well as a gap in her cut water* below the
bobstays.

*Where the bow touches the water.

A full-rigged bark, she was painted black. The vessel was a fairly able craft, though out of repair and carrying a rusty suit of sails. She appeared to have but a single deck with a deep waist, the poop extending to the main hatchway, with a netting around it. Her topgallant forecastle was open, with the forward house built around the foremast. She carried one quarterboat and a longboat stowed amidships, bottom up. *Tacony* was her name, and she hailed from Egg Island Harbor. At the moment she was sailing from Port Royal to Philadelphia.

Armed with revolvers and cutlasses, a boarding crew led by Read clambered over her side. None of them wore uniforms. Taking over the *Tacony*, Read made prisoners of Captain Munday and his crew.

Lieutenant Read then inspected his prize and soon decided that for his purpose the *Tacony* was far superior to the square-rigger. Returning to the *Clarence*, he ordered all hands to transfer the dummy guns to the *Tacony* and take all their personal belongings as well.

While the transfer was going on, the schooner *Stewart* was sighted coming down wind. Drawing closer, she stood near the *Clarence*, falling in with Lieutenant Read's strategy, and an hour later the schooner became the next victim of the Southerner.

As Lieutenant Read had seventy-five prisoners from his five prizes, he decided to place them on the *Stewart*, liberating her on a bond for $7000, payable to the president of the Confederate States thirty days after the signing of a treaty of peace.

The seizure and transfer of prisoners took several hours, and it was noon before the *Stewart* got under way, heading directly for the Capes of the Delaware. Although Lieutenant Read was well aware that before twenty-four hours had passed the army in Washington would know the facts of the seizures and would dispatch vessels to hunt him down, not for a moment did this thought delay the work in hand.

On June 24, after capturing the packet ship *Shatemuc*, which was on her way to Boston with 350 passengers, Read bonded her for $150,000. Later the same day he captured the fishing schooner *Archer*, and put her crew aboard the *Shatemuc*. He then transferred all of his own crew as well as much material to the *Archer* and set the *Tacony** afire.

One of his crew was Robert Hunt, who years later told of going aboard the *Archer* that evening.

"Her crew were just about sitting down to a nice fish supper. Their captain asked us to join them, and as they had a first class chowder, beside some nice sounds and tongues cooked as they knew how to cook them, we accepted the invitation. After dark we transferred one six-pounder and such other articles as we needed from the *Tacony* to the *Archer*. We then set fire to the *Tacony* and staid by her until she burned to the water's edge and sank. She was a smart vessel and we were sorry to see her go. The next afternoon we anchored off Long wharf in Portland harbor. All hands were below, with the exception of a few hands knocking about the deck.

"Those below were employed making oakum balls and saturating them with turpentine, with which to set fire to the gunboats. At the last moment, when everything was in readiness and every man had received his instructions our engineer, Mr. Brown, informed Lieutenant Read that he did not feel competent to take charge of the Boston steamer's engine. Lieutenant Read then decided to capture the United States revenue cutter *Caleb Cushing* and put to sea again."

Indeed it was quite a situation in which Lieutenant Read found himself. There was the revenue cutter *Caleb Cushing*, a topsail schooner, with armament consisting of a thirty-two-pounder mounted on a pivot amidships and a brass twelve-pounder Dahlgren forward. Though the adventurers on the

---

*A Confederate sailor with Read later buried a treasure of $1800 at Haskell Island. According to legend a farmer on the island plowed up the gold around the year 1900.

Archer did not know it, the captain of the cutter had that very day died of heart failure, and the vessel was in charge of a young lieutenant with a short crew of fourteen men because all the others were ashore on detail or leave.

As Lieutenant Read lounged in apparently careless attitude on the deck of the *Archer*, scanning with his keen brown eyes the waterfront, the town rising in graceful outline against the western sky, he turned over in his mind his plan of campaign. The supreme moment had come. Here he was in an enemy's port, unsuspected.

He viewed the city he had dreamed of destroying just as Captain Henry Mowatt had done ninety-eight years before when the city was a town. The shipping he hoped to cut out or burn was at hand, and his men were below decks engaged in making balls of oakum and saturating them with turpentine.

The hours of that peaceful June evening were uneasy ones. He held another anxious consultation with Brown, the only engineer aboard, about attempting to cut out the New York steamer *Chesapeake*, or in the morning, on her arrival, the Boston steamer *Forest City*. Steam was not up on the *Chesapeake*, and Brown doubted if he could start her engines, or even those of the Boston steamer. Had there been another engineer in the party it might be done, but the task seemed beyond the powers of the third assistant engineer of the *Florida*. This took from Read one of the chief weapons with which he had hoped to strike. He did not blame Mr. Brown, but resigned the idea of cutting out either of the steamers, and with characteristic initiative, fell to other plans. The night was so calm and still he doubted if a boat could approach the gunboats without detection by the watchmen who guarded them, while fireballs thrown on board would in the absence of wind do small damage.

Giving up this project also, Read now turned his attention to the cutter and formulated a plan of action. The *Cushing* swung to one anchor, and the chain probably could be slipped. Her bulwarks were not so high but that a boarding party could go over them from boats at a single bound. It was apparent there was but one man on watch. Boats passing to and fro were not challenged. It would be easy to board the cutter.

After the plan was settled and the men had been given their instructions, time hung heavily on the hands of the adventurers on the *Archer*. There was a young moon spreading radiance over the harbor and the city. It would set about midnight, but until it went down nothing could be done. Another check was a small steamer plying back and forth between the city and Cushing's Island, where a party was in progress at the Ottawa House.

As the steamer passed on one of her trips, the sound of laughter and women's voices came across the water to the silent watchers on the fishing schooner's deck. It had been long since they had heard a woman's voice, and this, of all moments, was the last in which they cared to hear it. As Winfield Thompson stated, such reminders of the softer side of existence are not the sort of thing to stimulate a man to acts that perhaps will cost him his life.

Watching the dying moon, the men of the South waited until after midnight when the harbor lay in darkness. Then the word was passed in a whisper to carry out the commander's instructions for boarding the cutter. The two boats were brought alongside and silently manned. Each man took off his shoes. Care was taken to avoid stepping on the oars, as the smallest sound carried far over the glassy water.

With twelve men in each boat, including one of the prisoners for a pilot, the boats shoved off. Their tholepins had been muffled with rags and marlin,* and the men rowed the short distance between the schooner and the cutter without making

---

*Just as Paul Revere's oarsmen had softened their strokes generations before with a petticoat.

a splash as they carefully dipped their blades. Going slowly, they came up to the cutter from astern. The watch was forward, and by the time he challenged them the boats were close aboard. Hailing again, and getting no answer, the man ran aft, took a look at the approaching boats, and rushed down into the cabin to arouse the commanding officer, Lieutenant Dudley Davenport.

The lieutenant, his eyes heavy with sleep, reached the deck to find himself confronted by four men who pointed pistols at him and demanded his surrender. One of them was Lieutenant Read.

"Keep quiet, and we will not harm you. Make a noise and you are a dead man! You are a prisoner to the Confederate States of America."*

Lieutenant Davenport heard these words as two men seized his hands and put irons on them. He was powerless, for his vessel was already in the hands of the Confederate crew. They had found the main hatch open on reaching the cutter's deck. Springing down into the area where the crew lay asleep in their hammocks, in the dim light of a bulkhead lantern they had covered the men with pistols and made them prisoners. To put them in irons and gag them was the work of but a few minutes. Lieutenant Davenport was confined in his room.

Within five minutes after their arrival alongside the cutter the Confederates were in undisputed possession of the vessel, fore and aft. So silently and expeditiously had their work been done that not a sound made on board had carried across the water to the forts or the docks, or to any of the other vessels in port.

As soon as their prisoners were confined, the men from the *Archer* began getting the cutter under way. An attempt to slip the chain proved a failure, as a link could not be cut and no shackle was in sight. There was nothing to do but heave up the

*Statement of Lieutenant Davenport in the *Portland Advertiser.*

anchor. This took half an hour, the clink of the windlass sounding ominously loud to the anxious Confederates as the anchor came to the bow. There was not a breath of air, so the cutter, with two boats ahead, was slowly towed toward Hussey's Sound, a northern outlet of the harbor, not much used, by which the forts could be avoided. Cliff Island and Jewel Island were soon left behind.

By six in the morning, with the help of a light land breeze, she was at least four miles off the closest harbor islands. The land breeze grew fainter and fainter as the morning advanced, but about eight o'clock, after an interval of calm, a very light air was noticed.

At about the same time, Collector of Customs Jedediah Jewett was at breakfast when an excited messenger knocked at his front door. The messenger brought the intelligence that the cutter *Caleb Cushing* had put to sea in the night and could then be seen from the observatory on Munjoy's Hill. Lieutenant J. H. Merryman, of the revenue cutter service, had arrived that morning on the Boston boat to take command of the *Cushing*, and had seen the cutter at four A.M. standing out as she left Portland Harbor.

Collector Jewett at once decided that Lieutenant Davenport, who was of Southern birth, had seized the opportunity afforded by the death of the *Cushing*'s commander to run away with the cutter and turn her over to the Confederates. Jewett then did an excellent job of organizing a chase to capture the *Cushing*. Hastening to the custom house, he sent to the Boston and New York steamers, requesting that the craft be chartered to the government for the chase of the *Caleb Cushing*. Messengers were dispatched to Fort Preble, asking for troops to be put on the steamers. Another messenger went to a camp outside the city with a similar request. By this time the news had spread that an expedition was being formed to recapture the cutter. Citizens armed with swords and fowling pieces came running to the docks to volunteer their services. The mayor of the city, Captain Jacob McClellan, requisitioned from the state armory several pieces of ordnance and assisted in the embarkation himself.

As steam had to be got up on the *Chesapeake* and bales of cotton arranged along her sides to protect her engines and boilers, she was not ready as soon as the *Forest City*. The tide was low, and as this delayed the latter in taking on a detachment of the 17th U.S. Infantry at Fort Preble, it was nearly eleven o'clock before the steamer was able to leave the harbor. The *Chesapeake* got away about half an hour later. Two small tugs, the *Tiger* and *Uncle Sam*, also went out.*

While this flotilla was taking to sea, the *Cushing*, in the light southeasterly wind, was standing offshore on the port tack, making perhaps two knots through the water. Lieutenant Read was below. He had breakfasted with Mr. Brown, and Lieutenant Davenport had been their guest. At breakfast Lieutenant Read, knowing Lieutenant Davenport to be a Southern man, had said:

"I am sorry, Lieutenant, to meet you under these circumstances, but this is one of the fortunes of war. You, being a Southern man, ought to be ashamed of yourself."

Choosing to ignore this pointed remark on his loyalty to the South, Lieutenant Davenport replied:

"You have acted humanely, sir, and in case we are taken I'll represent you favorably to the United States authorities."

All morning the Confederates had been searching the *Cush-*

---

*The *Forest City* carried 28 men of the 17th U.S. Infantry under Captain N. Prime, with one 6-pounder fieldpiece, one 12-pounder and ammunition. Muskets were furnished from Fort Preble to about 40 citizens on this steamer which carried about 200 men in all. On the *Chesapeake* was a detachment of 27 men from Company G of the 7th Maine Volunteers. Captain Henry Warren was in charge of two brass 6-pounders from the State Arsenal and about 50 armed citizens, including several old men-of-warsmen, and even a fighting parson, for, according to a local paper, "Rev. Mr. Waldron, of the Park Street Church, rendered valuable service in helping to make cartridges."

ing fore and aft for ammunition to serve the guns in case of pursuit. The final throw of the dice would be made when a chase began, and its success depended on supporting it with shot from the cutter's battery. They found four hundred pounds of powder, but only five shot. The first of these was discovered in a potato locker, and others in various out-of-the-way places, showing that they were not part of the regular supply of the ship. Demands had been made on Lieutenant Davenport and the crew to reveal the location of the shot locker, but all hands declared that only the day before they had received orders to join in the pursuit of the *Tacony*, and had taken on powder but not shot and shell. This story the Confederates eventually believed. They failed to find a locker containing more than ninety solid shot for the cutter's thirty-two-pounder.

Confederate crewman Robert Hunt gave the following account of what happened next:

"Our little breeze died away, and Read ordered all hands below to get what rest they could. While I was looking astern I saw what looked to be a steamer coming out, and, as I thought, heading for us. I called Read, who came on deck, and, after looking at her awhile, said he guessed it was the Boston steamer bound out. He went below again, telling me to keep an eye on her. I shortly discovered another steamer astern of her, also coming out, and, on looking through the glasses, saw a crowd of soldiers on the upper deck. I immediately called our commander. On his reaching the deck, after one glance at the steamer, he called all hands to clear for action. The thirty-two-pounder was loaded and the order given to put the helm hard down, the gunner and crew in the meantime training the gun to get a range on the nearest steamer. The cutter would not mind her helm.

" 'Hard down!' shouted Read, jumping toward the helm.

" 'Hard down it is,' I answered.

" 'Oh, for a six-knot breeze and a few shot or shell!' cried

Read, 'we would show them some fun!'

"The steamers were directly in our wake, and when Read saw we could not get an effective shot at them he said: 'We will give them a scare, anyhow!'

"The gun was trained as far aft as possible, and the order given to fire. When the smoke cleared away both steamers were broadside to, as if turning back, and we gave a yell, and shouted, 'load her up again!' But we had nothing to load her with. Read at once gave orders to set fire to the cutter and abandon her.

"The prisoners were brought on deck, put in two boats, given the key to their irons, and turned adrift. I jumped down into the cabin and proceeded to break up the furniture and collect the bedding to set on fire. When the order was given to set fire, I struck a match, and in an instant the whole cabin seemed on fire. I rushed for the companionway, and when I reached the deck I was pretty badly scorched—eyebrows, lashes and mustache singed, and face and hands pretty well blistered. At this time all hands were in the boats, with the exception of the gunner and myself. He had gathered up a lot of scrap iron, nails, spikes, etc., with which he had loaded the gun for a parting shot. Although the steamers were dead astern and not within three or four points of the range of the gun, they both stopped when the last shot was fired.

"We pulled away from the cutter and lay on our oars, knowing that it would be useless to try to get away. Read ordered us to throw our arms overboard, and every man stood up in the boats, unbuckled his belt, to which were attached his revolver and cutlass, and dropped it over the side. Read then produced a shot-bag of specie which he divided among us. Our next act was to tie a white handkerchief to our boat hook and await our fate.

"The first steamer had been steering directly for us from the time we abandoned the cutter. The other stopped to pick up the crew of the cutter. We noticed that when the first steamer got near us, a detachment of soldiers on the upper deck had their muskets aimed directly at us, as if about to fire, but an officer sprang in front of them with a drawn sword and they at once came to shoulder.

"We were ordered alongside, a rope was thrown to us, and we were taken on board. One man at a time was allowed to come over the side. He was searched, and then his arms tied behind his back with a piece of rattling stuff, and he was placed under guard before another was taken on board."

Meanwhile two boatloads of excited volunteers had started from the *Forest City* with the intention of boarding the cutter. The first crew expected to engage the Confederates, but on seeing the vessel in flames turned back.* The second were bent on subduing the fire with buckets. By the time they got alongside, they gave up the job, contenting themselves with taking away a small boat half full of water that lay alongside. The man who got into the boat had no knife to cut the painter, and the time he took in untying it seemed an age to the others, who felt somewhat uncomfortable with red hot cinders and bits of burning sails and rigging falling on them, and the cutter's magazine likely to explode at any moment.*

While the volunteer crews were returning to their steamer, the fire reached the cutter's magazine at 1:48 P.M., and there was a terrific explosion that shook the little fleet standing by, causing the surface of the sea to boil. The whole deck of the vessel seemed to fly upward. A burst of flame and a vast column of smoke rose from her shattered hull. Fragments of iron, blackened timbers, bits of plank and spars, and innumerable cinders flew out and fell into the sea. Staggering as she went, the *Cushing* settled by the stern and disappeared. One of her spars, dislodged by the explosion, came up in the whirlpool. After rising heel uppermost fifteen or twenty feet, the spar

*Memoirs of Captain Benjamin J. Willard, Portland.
* *Portland Argus*, June 29, 1863.

slowly disappeared, drawn down by a piece of rigging attaching it to the wreck. The *Cushing* sank in thirty-three fathoms, about ten or twelve miles south-southeast from the outer islands.*

Fisherman Titcomb, who had been held a prisoner on the *Cushing*, told the captors of Lieutenant Read that the *Archer* was off to the eastward. She had three men on board, including another fisherman. Later she was found and towed to Portland and, with the steamers, was received by the people with the ringing of bells, firing of guns, and other demonstrations of popular joy over the downfall of the "rebel pirates."

When the *Archer* was searched, chronometers, nautical instruments, charts, books, chests, and various other items from Lieutenant Read's prizes were found on board, without ammunition, all of which had been expended aboard the *Tacony*—about twenty-five muskets, and some cutlasses. Lieutenant Read's carpetbag, containing his commission, journal, the logs of his cruise, letters, and other papers, was also discovered and turned over to government representatives at Portland.

While the schooner was being searched, an idler on deck picked up a musket and accidentally discharged it, mortally wounding Mr. Jacob Gould, a stevedore employed in unloading the vessel. This was the only life lost in connection with the raid of Lieutenant Read and his men.

After being imprisoned in the guardhouse at Fort Preble, Lieutenant Read and his crew were transferred to Fort Warren in Boston Harbor.

Lieutenant Joseph W. Alexander, another Confederate prisoner at Fort Warren, wrote an account of what occurred after Read's arrival in Boston Harbor.

"Fort Warren was commanded by Colonel Dimmick and was garrisoned by some local Massachusetts troops. The offic-

*It is said that scuba divers visited the sunken *Cushing* several years ago.

ers and men always treated us kindly. At first we were allowed to purchase anything we wished, and for a while our friends in Baltimore and some in Boston sent us many things, clothing and eatables; but after a time, acting under orders received from Washington, we were not allowed to buy anything and had only the rations usually allowed prisoners, which were neither plentiful nor inviting. The privilege of purchasing provisions was taken from us, it was said, in retaliation for the treatment the Federal prisoners received at the hands of the Confederates; but this matter has been fully discussed and will not be dwelt on here. After this the underground railway brought us such things as we were able to pay enormously for.

"Besides the prisoners taken on the *Atlanta*, there were the officers and crew of the *Tacony* and some political prisoners and blockade-runners confined in Fort Warren. We were kept in the casemates under the main battery. In the daytime we were allowed to take exercise on the pavements in front of our quarters, but after sundown we were locked in the casemates, and sentinels placed in front of our doors. Four of us, Lieutenant C. W. Read of the *Tacony* (a prize vessel converted into a Confederate naval boat); Lieutenant of Marines James Thurston of the *Atlanta*; Reid Sanders, a political prisoner from Kentucky;* and myself determined to escape. Many plans were suggested and discussed, but none seemed feasible. Indeed, situated as we were on an island, and strictly guarded day and night, with sentinels stationed in front of our doors, confined within solid masonry constructed to resist the shot from the heaviest guns, it seemed impossible to escape; and yet escape was easily accomplished.

"In the basement under the room in which we were confined was a pump where we obtained our water, and in the outer wall of this basement were two openings called musketry loopholes.

---

*Sanders was actually a major in the Confederate Army. A relative, also named Reid Sanders, later lived in Quincy, Massachusetts.

These were something over six feet high, two or three feet wide at the inside of the wall, and gradually sloping to a point, so that at the outer side of the wall they were only a little over seven inches wide. One day, while bathing, the thought struck me that I could get through this hole, and I immediately tried it. I found that by turning my head so as to look over my shoulder, I could get through, but with my clothes on I could not get my body through. Stripping off my clothes, I tried again, and found I could squeeze through, though it was hard to do it. This discovery was made known to the other three, and each one found he could get through quite easily, as I was the largest one of the party. No time was lost after this in getting ready for our escape."

On Sunday night, August 16, 1863, the four Southerners made an attempt to flee. A wild northeaster was blowing, and the night was very dark. After tying together the rope from their canvas bags, they crawled through the loophole and dropped down to the level of the dry moat, located between the main and water batteries. After carefully surveying the situation they walked across the open space in the direction of a wooden target which stood on the beach a few rods from the thicket.

Lieutenant Alexander continues:

"We made our way cautiously over the water battery and then through the grass towards the sea-wall, where we found, as we expected and feared, that sentinels were posted. These would walk backwards and forwards on the wall, and when they met they would turn and walk off in the opposite directions. Keeping close to the ground we would approach the walls when they were walking from each other, and remain quiet after they turned and were coming together.

"Finally we succeeded in passing between them while their backs were towards us, and got into the water close to the wall, lying down with our heads against the wall, and our feet in the water. Finding the sea very rough and the wind high, after a considerable time we concluded it would be very dangerous to try to swim at that time; so we watched our chance and succeeded in regaining our quarters, as our friends inside, by our direction, had left the rope hanging down from the loop-hole so that we could go back if for any reason we could not succeed in getting off the island.

"Only a few of the prisoners knew we had been out. Most of them ridiculed the idea that anyone could get through so small a hole. A smart little midshipman, seeing our wet clothes, *tasted,* and finding them *salt,* was convinced.

"The failure of our first attempt did not discourage us. Lieutenant Read suggested that two of his men, good swimmers and very reliable, be allowed to go with us. He talked with them, and they readily agreed to accompany us."

The two men were N. B. Pryde and a former sailor of the U.S. Navy, Thomas Sherman. Across on Lovell's Island was a sailboat tied on the shore which was the property of the island resident Barber. It was arranged for the two new men to escape through the slits in their part of the fort, meet the others, and then swim across the narrows which separate the two islands. Once on Lovell's Island they would get the boat and sail it back to pick up the other four men.

When the night of August 19 began dark and threatening, almost every prisoner knew that the break would be attempted. At about 9:15 P.M. the four men started to climb out of the casemates. All was quiet until Lieutenant Alexander inadvertently knocked over a bottle, which crashed on the granite with a noise that it was feared must have been heard by the guard at the main sallyport. There was a challenge from the sentry; the prisoners shivered.

Alexander looked over at the drawbridge that ran across the moat and found that the challenge had merely been addressed to an officer passing into the sallyport. Because of the rising

Portland Head Light, always visited by the Flying Santa. (Pt. I, Ch. 1)

Keeper Kilt of Portland Head Light playing on giant checkerboard with Anna-Myrle Snow. (Pt. I, Ch. 1)

Flying Santa plane lands in snowstorm at Portland Airport with package for Portland Head Light. (Pt. I, Ch. 1) PHOTO BY FREDERICK G. S. CLOW

The McGuire shipwreck inscription at Portland Head Light. (Pt. I, Ch. 1)

Cape Elizabeth Light, photograph by the author during Flying Santa trip.
(Pt. I, Ch. 2)

The author paddling ashore at Halfway Rock Light. (Pt. I, Ch. 3)

Keeper Horace A. Leverett of Halfway Rock Light rowing Anna-Myrle Snow and Dorothy Snow ashore at the Casco Bay Ledge. (Pt. I, Ch. 3)

Colonel Alexander Scammell, for whom Fort Scammell was named. (Pt. I, Ch. 6)

Awesome granite staircase at Fort Scammell on House Island. (Pt. I, Ch. 6) COURTESY OF HASTY THOMPSON

Captain Robert A. Lee of Coast Guard tells story of the fight between the *Boxer* and the *Enterprise* as the author holds sword of surrender. Captain Blythe's grave is at left, Captain Burrows' is in center. (Pt. II, Ch. 2)

PHOTO BY FREDERICK G. S. CLOW

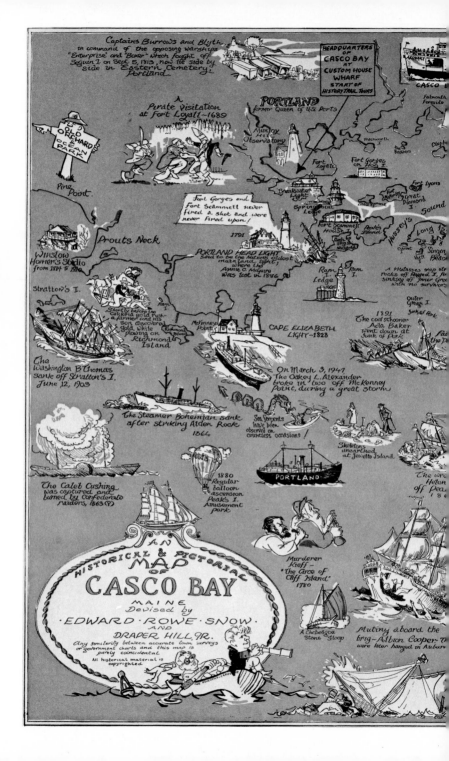

FREEPORT

Casco Castle near South Freeport

Porter's Landing

Ames cut masts British ships

Royal River

Barlot

BRUNSWICK

Bowdoin College Established 1794

Massachusetts Hall 1802

Wolf Neck

CROWSTOWN

Dutch River

Bowman

Crab I.

Wilson's Point

Stopping point of an Around the World Flight 1924

Cousins I.

Little John's I.

Moshier Island

Little Cabins

Mouse I.

Mere point Neck

Little Moses

Bustins I.

Sow & Pigs

French I.

Irony I.

Cedar I.

Will's I.

Birch I.

Whito I.

Scrag I.

Chebeague I.

Upper Green I.

The fair cows of Lower Goose

Lower Goose

Little Goose

The Stings

Stony I.

Shelter I.

Crow I.

Goose Nest

Little Hog I.

The funeral of the "witch" of Harpswell Neck

Little Bangs

Bethmoon

Whaleboats

Little Iron I.

Sebascodegan Island

Neck

Three makers lost 1957

Eagle Island Summer home of Admiral Peary

Potts Harbor

Bush I.

Orr's Island

Oak Point

Quahog Bay

Long Cove

Birch I.

Long Reach

The Monument erected in Harpswell Cutters built in 1827

Bailey I.

Mark Island

Turnip I.

1874 Hoodlums recorded at Lowell Cove

BEACH POINT Sheep Wash

The Dash Casco Bay's Flying Dutchman

Cedar Ledges

Elm Islands

Two Bush I.

A pot of Gold discovered by John Wilson

Pond I.

Motorhouse Hill

Ragged Island Summer home of poetess Edna St Vincent Millay. Elijah Kellogg, writer of boys books, called it Elm I.

N

W   E

S

Giant's Stairway Bailey Island

The Schooner Sheffield Gloucester was lost at Pond I.

Sand Island

Cape Small

A Cob-work bridge connects Orr's I. and Bailey I. unique in the United States.

Seawall Beach

Black Rocks

Island"-heroine Harriet Beecher Stowe, "Uncle Tom's Cabin"

The Grotto, Orr's Island

The excursion Steamer City of Rockland crashed on rocks off SEAWALL BEACH – April 26, 1909

CITY OF ROCKLAND

The Clara Clarita lost off Stage I. Nov 11, 1910

A revenue cutter, Dobbin, captures a sloop, manned by Confederate prisoners from Fort Warren, August, 1863

The Don lost in June, 1941, with 34 aboard a greatest Casco Bay Mystery!

SEGUIN LIGHT 1795

Seguin I.

...castle crashed on ...nd, Dec 13, 1822. 137 ...rown, wrecked ...veral.

Speeding to her doom as predicted in the vision of Pilot Silas Cook's daughter, the proud ship Hanover goes down Nov 9, 1849 after sighting Seguin light. All 21 were drowned, but a small dog was saved. The incident was mentioned in "The Pearl of Orr's Island."

During the War of 1812, the American frigate Enterprise defeated the British Boxer far off Seguin I. on Sept. 5, 1813.

Peter McLaughlin of Casco Bay Lines explains to the author how the present site of the Custom House Wharf escaped the Great Fire of 1866. (Pt. II, Ch. 4) PHOTO BY FREDERICK G. S. CLOW

Lieutenant Charles W. Read, seated fourth from right, as a prisoner at Fort Warren after his capture in Casco Bay. He was later released, was again captured and returned to Fort Warren. (Pt. II, Ch. 3)

The *Novadoc,* lost with all hands in the *Oakey Alexander* Gale in 1947, probably near Halfway Rock. (Pt. II, Ch. 9) PHOTO BY WILLIAM F. CURREN, JR.

Dramatic moment when the breeches buoy was attached to the *Oakey L. Alexander,* on March 3, 1947, at McKenny's Point, Cape Elizabeth. (Pt. II, Ch. 9)

Right: Flying Santa greeting residents at a Casco Bay island. PHOTO BY FREDERICK G. S. CLOW

Johanna von Tiling and her father in 1957 at Cliff Island. (Pt. V, Ch. 2)

Emita II at Bailey Island Landing, Casco Bay, where 1963 canoe trip began. (Pt. V, Ch. 5)

The author at wheel of veteran steamer *Sabino,* which ran thousands of miles in Casco Bay. PHOTO BY DICK NAKASHIAN

Chester Shea, wearing ancient helmet of Ferdinand Gorges, shakes hands with Stanley Burrows of Long Island. (Pt. V, Ch. 7) PHOTO BY FREDERICK G. S. CLOW

The famous profile of the Ancient Lady at Cushing Island, called by some the Old Man. The features of the face can clearly be seen above the bust of the woman.

wind the crash had not been heard. With great relief the four men now climbed down into the moat and made for the meeting place at the top of the cover face. Prydé and Sherman were waiting for them, having successfully escaped from the embrasure in their part of the bastion.

It was then agreed that Read and Sanders should wait in the shelter of the cover face while the four others made their way down to the shore. Evading the sentries by the same method as before, the four men reached the edge of the water. The two swimmers stripped off their clothing, and after a word of farewell, plunged into the dark waters. That farewell, as far as is known, was the last ever heard from them. F. A. Boles, writing of the incident in 1864, said that nothing had been learned of the two swimmers up to that time.

This disappearance of Prydé and Sherman is one of the strangest incidents in the history of Fort Warren. The men simply vanished. After the report was made that they had swum away to freedom, it was assumed by some that they had reached the South. Investigation after the war, however, revealed that they had not been heard from since that night of August 19, 1863, when they had left the island. As no bodies ever washed ashore in the vicinity of their escape, their disappearance will always remain an unsolved mystery.

Lieutenant Alexander reports further:

"Waiting, as it seemed to us for hours, and the sailors not returning, Thurston and I determined that we would swim over to the island on which the lighthouse stood, get a boat and return for Read and Sanders, neither of whom, being poor swimmers, was willing to take the risk. Close to the shore where we passed to the water was a target, made of white pine and very light. The garrison used this target to practice on, and after consulting together we, Thurston and I, determined to use it to float our clothes over on, shoving it ahead of us as we swam.

"Watching our chance, we pulled it down and got it into the

water while the sentinels were on their outward trip; and it came very near being the means of defeating our plan; for before we could get away they came together again, right over our heads, on the sea-wall, and began to talk on indifferent subjects, and continued for some time. Finally one said to the other, *"Where is the target?* Wasn't it here when we came on post?" "Yes," was the reply. "Where can it be?" They came to the edge of the wall, and looked over. It was very dark in the shadow, and we lay close together, barely breathing.

" 'I believe I see something down here in the water,' said one. 'Stick your bayonet into it and see what it is,' said the other. The sentinel lowered the muzzle of his musket, and shoved it slowly towards Read's breast, directly under him. The point finally rested on his *chest!* He never moved a muscle, but remained perfectly quiet. That was the bravest thing I saw during the four years of the war.

"But it was only for a moment. The man pulled his gun up, remarking, 'I am not going to stick my bayonet into salt water.' After this they stood for what seemed to us an age, and discussed the disappearance of the target, finally concluding that the 'spirits had taken it away.' Then they separated and moved off, widening the distance between us.

"Now was our chance. Tying our clothes to the target, we pushed it off and headed for the shore of the island, which lay some distance from the fort. Though it was August the water seemed as cold as ice. Want of exercise had weakened us, and though we made apparently good progress, it seemed hours that we were in the water, and the tide swept us down all the time.

"There was a lighthouse* on an island opposite the lower end of the island on which the fort was built. We kept this light a little to the right of us as we swam, and finally, after a long time —it seemed hours—we stopped for a moment, letting our feet

*Bug Light or the Narrows Beacon.

sink under us. We both touched bottom at the same time, and straightening up, we waded ashore, pulling the target after us. We were almost frozen, but as soon as we had put the target some little distance from the water we set out along the shore to look for a boat, keeping together for fear we might not be able to find each other without a noise, if we separated, and not knowing whether or not anyone lived on the island. After a long time we came upon a small fishing boat, which had been dragged up on the beach, and anchored so as to keep it in place.

"We pulled the anchor up to the bow of the boat, and secured it; then we tried to shove the boat into the water. It was so small that we ought to have launched it easily; yet after moving it a certain distance, we could get it no further. I cannot tell how long we were at this business, but it was a long time. Finally, trying to see what kept the boat from moving, we found there was a second anchor over the stern. Cutting the rope which held the boat, we shoved it into the water, and getting on board we hoisted the sail and steered over towards the fort, intending to take down the sail when we got nearer and pull in for Read and Sanders. It had been getting lighter for some time, but was not quite daylight. We stood on, but did not dare to get too near, for fear of exciting the suspicion of the sentinels, whom we could see very plainly. Finally, as it got lighter and lighter, we reluctantly turned the boat's head toward the sea, as we could plainly see that Read and Sanders had left and were perhaps back in the casemates, having given us up. It was a sad disappointment to us. I believe we could have got them off, if we could have launched the boat without delay.

"I afterwards learned that, waiting till nearly daylight, they attempted to return to the casemates; but they waited too long, and were discovered and put in close confinement."

Alexander and Thurston sailed right up the Massachusetts coast, stopping at both Rockport and Rye Beach for food and clothing. Setting their course for St. John, they were sailing through Casco Bay, between Cliff Island and Jewel Island, when they were chased and captured by the revenue cutter *R. M. Dobbin*. They were taken to the Portland jail, where people came to see the "rebels from Fort Warren" as if they were animals in a zoo. They left Portland forever on September 7, 1863, not quite three weeks from the time of their escape, and finally arrived under guard back at Fort Warren.

Eventually Read left Fort Warren when he was exchanged for a Northern officer who had been captured by the South. He entered the Confederate Navy again, receiving the rank of commander. In January, 1865, he set out to destroy the monitor *Onondaga*, but his mission failed. Again, on February 10, he attempted to clear the James River and blow up Yankee craft there, but this effort also failed.

Read's final exploit actually occurred after Lee's surrender, when he planned to torpedo the Union craft *Fearnaught*. The torpedo boom snapped, and Read was forced to cut the guy ropes, sinking the torpedo. There were three hundred barrels of powder aboard the *Fearnaught*, and Read and his men would have been blown to pieces had his mission succeeded.

Read was forced to surrender to the Union forces, and again arrived as a prisoner at Fort Warren on May 10. There he soon learned that his old quarters were being readied for the arrival of Vice-President of the Confederate States Alexander Hamilton Stephens, an event that occurred on May 25, 1865.

In 1904 a classmate of Read's, Admiral W. S. Schley, stated that Charles Read had "sublime courage, conspicuous dash, and great originality, and was aggressive in all that he did. He won fame as have all who possessed those qualities."

In a victorious cause Charles W. Read would have won undying fame. His abilities were singularly like those of Paul Jones, and his achievements in destroying commerce of a similar nature. Unlike Jones, he was denied the glory of a successful sea fight, though his courage was such there can be no doubt he would have acquitted himself with credit. Inasmuch as the struggle in which he played an important part was between brethren of the same land, it is perhaps just as well he did not achieve greatness in battle. His activities, however, entitle him to credit for tireless energy, unbounded enthusiasm, and almost reckless bravery. He was forever making plans for furthering his cause, and nothing served to dampen his ardor.

4

The Portland Fire of 1866

More than ninety years had elapsed after the awesome destruction of Falmouth* by the notorious British commander Captain Henry Mowatt when the area was hit by another disastrous conflagration. The first burning of the city was deliberate. Mowatt destroyed Falmouth by gunpowder and torch during the Revolutionary War, but the second and even more overwhelming catastrophe was caused by accident.

In 1834 in Springfield, Massachusetts, an event of far-reaching importance occurred. Alonzo Phillips discovered an easy way of making and lighting matches. He patented his invention the following year. On July 4, 1866, this led to disaster for Portland.

On that Wednesday a boy, who shall be nameless, was playing in the Deguio Boatyard on Commercial Street on the Portland waterfront. He lighted a Phillips match, touched it to a firecracker, and then dropped the match into a pile of shavings, which quickly caught fire.

*Falmouth officially became known as Portland on July 4, 1786.

The flames spread rapidly in the boatyard, which was soon totally ablaze. I can do no better than quote from the Portland *Daily Press*, which on Friday morning, July 6, was published by F. G. Rich, a job printer. Every other printing press in the entire city of Portland had been consumed by the flames.

"Our city was visited on Wednesday by one of the most destructive fires that has ever occurred in the United States. It commenced at half past four o'clock, Wednesday afternoon, and continues burning at the time of writing this, 3 o'clock, Thursday afternoon.

"The fire commenced in the Deguio's boat shop on Commercial [s]treet and was caused by a lad's firing a cracker among some shavings on the outside of the building, which set them on fire. The flames quickly communicated to the interior of the building which, in a few minutes, was all a blaze, and the adjoining building, corner of Maple and Commercial streets also caught fire and rapidly burned.

"There was a high wind prevailing at the time and the flames and cinders were blown directly upon the extensive buildings of the Portland Sugar House Company. Soon these were all on fire, and the large foundries of Messrs. C. Staples & Son, and N. P. Richardson on Commercial street caught and though the most strenuous exertions were made to save them they were entirely destroyed.

"From these points the fire rapidly extended to York, Maple, and the lower part of Danforth streets to Centre St., destroying everything. From Centre street it extended to Cotton street, thence to Cross street, running up that street to Middle street and extending down Middle street to Temple and from Temple to Exchange street. From Exchange St.—from Fore Street to the City Hall, and then down Myrtle to Cumberland street— from these bounds to India street, every building, save the Custom House is destroyed—on the north side of Fore street, both sides of Congress street, all on the south side of Cumberland street from Myrtle to Washington streets, except the Radford house on the corner of Pearl and Cumberland, together with all the buildings on the intersecting cross streets.

"The fire crossed Washington street and destroyed a large number of buildings between that point and North street.

"The flames blew over into Oxford street, and several dwelling houses were destroyed, and the flames are still raging.

"It is estimated that 1,500 buildings—dwelling houses, shops, &c., have been destroyed. The loss is estimated, roughly, at from ten to twelve millions of dollars. So far as we have been able to learn there is insurance for upwards of $4,000,000. The amount is undoubtedly greater, but we have not been furnished with information beyond that sum.

"As to the names of the sufferers it is utterly impossible at this moment to give them. The heaviest losers are Hon. John B. Brown & Sons and Messrs. Churchill, Brown & Mauson, who estimate their loss at about $1,000,000, on which there is insurance to the amount of $600,000. This does not include the private buildings owned by Mr. Brown.

"Eight Churches were destroyed: 1st Baptist, Federal street; St. Stephen's Episcopalian, Pearl street; 2d Parish, Middle street; Pearl Street Universalist, Pearl street; Chapel of the Immaculate Conception, Catholic, Cumberland street; Swedenborgian, Congress street; Bethel, Fore street; 3d Parish, Congress street.

"Seven Hotels were destroyed—Elm, International, American, Commercial, Franklin, Kingsbury House and Sturdevant House.

"The unfinished marble hotel erected by the late Hon. John M. Wood, was burned down. The beautiful mansion of Mrs. Wood shared the same fate.

"Every newspaper office in the city was destroyed. There is no exception.—The Argus, Advertiser, Press, Mirror, Transcript, Zion's Advocate and Price Current printing offices are gone.

"All the banks in the city, viz: 1st National, 2d National, National Traders', Casco National, Canal National, Merchants' National, and Cumberland National, were destroyed.

"Every lawyers' office in the city was burned down. We believe there is not a single exception.

"Great hopes were entertained that our beautiful City Hall would escape, but it is a mere shell now.

"The building occupied by the Custom House and Postoffice was considered fireproof. But the flames crept into the upper part of the building, occupied as Court Room, and the interior was badly damaged. The Postoffice part was not so much damaged and the mails were regularly made up there Thursday.— Judge Clifford lost a part of his valuable law library, and Judge Fox lost the whole of his, which he had removed there but a few days previously.

"From the point where the fire commenced to the extreme point to which it extended, running from South to North, the distance is more than one mile. The width of the swath of the devastation from East to West is about one third of a mile, extending from Fore [s]treet to Cumberland street. The area of the burnt district can be easily marked out upon the plan of the city. Probably 200 acres of territory is burned over.—The following is the situation in the several streets.

"The most valuable articles in the vaults of the banks were removed, but the books and papers were left. None of the vaults have been opened as yet, but the cashiers have no doubt that all their contents are safe.

"PROPERTY DESTROYED AFTER BEING REMOVED

"It was considered by every one that the City Hall would pass unscathed and consequently furniture and valuable articles were carried there for security.—When the fire caught on the building there was hardly time to remove them and a large portion was destroyed.

"Many persons also removed their furniture and goods to what they considered safe places; but the fire reached and destroyed them before the owners were aware of it."

And so it was that Portland endured her second great holocaust in ninety years. As one man expressed it, it was hard to "see the fruits of so many years of patient endeavor wasted in a few hours," but the courage with which they faced the fact of destruction "admits the misfortune in all its magnitude, and sets promptly to repair it."

One third of the territorial surface of the city was desolated, together with a large part of Portland's business section. Half the population of the city were turned out of their homes without warning, and the "sudden dissolution of the solid piles of brick and stone" was an unbelievable nightmare.

However, some of the old city survived to provide a basis for the new. Several buildings were preserved, including the United States Hotel, Mr. Tolford's store, and the business establishment of D. F. Emery & Sons. Commercial Street suffered comparatively little, and the West Indian and coastwise trade was not affected. Although the famed Athenaeum Library was destroyed, the Public Library soon took its place, and the Natural History Society, which then had twice lost its entire collection, eventually resumed activity.

Portland recovered much faster than even its most optimistic citizens dreamed possible. In the holocaust, despite the extent of the disaster, not a life was lost. Immediately after the fire, tents sprang up to shelter the homeless, and contributions of provisions, clothing, money, and building materials came from everywhere.

Rebuilding began, with plans for the future included. Narrow streets were widened and crooked ones were straightened where it was at all practical. Portland today, although she no longer reigns "supreme as the Queen of American Ports," maintains her position as preeminent along the Maine coast, a triumph over the disaster that caused Henry Wadsworth Longfellow to say as he viewed his beloved city in ruins, "Desolation, desolation, desolation!"

5

The Loss of the *Hanover*

On a bright sunny day in the year 1849 the ship *Hanover* could be seen by many Casco Bay islanders in the general vicinity of Seguin Island Light. The residents of the nearby shoreline had just witnessed the end of a terrible three-day easterly hurricane. They watched with uneasiness as the *Hanover* backed and filled several times, as though the Maine-born master might be awaiting the ideal moment at high tide to make his final decision.

Across on Orr's Island two people were sitting in a one-horse shay, one "an old man, with the peculiarly hard but impressive physiognomy" that characterizes the seafaring population of the New England shores. By his side sat a girl of twenty-two, who had heard that her husband's ship, the *Hanover*, had been sighted, and had driven across to the headland with her older companion to watch the craft.

I can do no better at this point than to ask Harriet Beecher Stowe to continue the tale of the unfortunate ship *Hanover*.

The scenery of the road along which the two were riding was wild and bare. Only savins and mulleins, with their dark pyramids or white spires of velvet leaves, diversified the sandy wayside; but out at sea was a wide sweep of blue, reaching far to the open ocean, which lay rolling, tossing and breaking into white caps of foam in the bright sunshine. For two or three days a northeast storm had been raging, and the sea was in all the commotion which such a general upturning creates.

The two travelers reached a point of elevated land, where they paused a moment, and the man drew up the jogging, stiff-jointed old farm-horse, and raised himself upon his feet to look out at the prospect.

There might be seen in the distance the blue Kennebec sweeping out toward the ocean through its picturesque rocky shores, decked with cedars and other dusky evergreens, which were illuminated by the orange and flame-colored trees of Indian summer. Here and there scarlet creepers swung long trailing garlands over the faces of the dark rock, and fringes of goldenrod above swayed with the brisk blowing wind that was driving the blue waters seaward, in face of the up-coming ocean tide,—a conflict which caused them to rise in great foam-crested waves. There are two channels into this river from the open sea, navigable for ships which are coming into the city of Bath; one is broad and shallow, the other narrow and deep, and these are divided by a steep ledge of rocks.

Where the spectators of this scene were sitting, they could see in the distance a ship borne with tremendous force by the rising tide into the mouth of the river, and encountering a northwest wind which had succeeded the gale, as northwest winds often do on this coast. The ship, from what might be observed in the distance, seemed struggling to make the wider channel, but was constantly driven off by the baffling force of the wind.

"There she is, Naomi," said the old fisherman, eagerly,

to his companion, "coming right in." The young woman was one of the sort that never start, and never exclaim, but with all deeper emotions grow still. The color slowly mounted into her cheek, her lips parted, and her eyes dilated with a wide, bright expression; her breathing came in thick gasps, but she said nothing.

The old fisherman stood up in the wagon, his coarse butternut-colored coat-flaps fluttering and snapping in the breeze, while his interest seemed to be so intense in the efforts of the ship that he made involuntary and eager movements as if to direct her course. A moment passed, and his keen, practiced eye discovered a change in her movements, for he cried out involuntarily,—

"*Don't* take the narrow channel to-day!" and a moment after, "O Lord! O Lord! have mercy,—there they go! Look! Look! Look!"

And, in fact, the ship rose on a great wave clear out of the water, and the next second seemed to leap with a desperate plunge into the narrow passage; for a moment there was a shivering of the masts and rigging, and she went down and was gone.

"They're split to pieces!" cried the fisherman. "Oh, my poor girl—my poor girl—they're gone! O Lord, have mercy!"

The woman lifted up no voice, but, as one who has been shot through the heart falls with no cry, she fell back,—a mist rose over her great mournful eyes,—she had fainted.

The story of this wreck of a home-bound ship just entering the harbor is yet told in many a family on this coast. A few hours after, the unfortunate crew were washed ashore in all the joyous holiday rig in which they had attired themselves that morning to go to their sisters, wives, and mothers.

The body of the young sea captain, is now lying in the old-fashioned parlor of his Orr's Island home.

Let us enter the dark front-door. We feel our way to the right, where a solitary ray of light comes from the chink of a half-opened door. Here is the front room of the house, set apart as its place of especial social hilarity and sanctity, —the "best room," with its low studded walls, white dimity window-curtains, rag carpet, and polished wood chairs. It is now lit by the dim gleam of a solitary tallow candle, which seems in the gloom to make only a feeble circle of light around itself, leaving all the rest of the apartment in shadow.

In the center of the room, stretched upon a table, and covered partially by a sea-cloak, lies the body of a man of twenty-five,—lies, too, evidently as one of whom it is written, "He shall return to his house no more, neither shall his place know him any more."

A splendid manhood has suddenly been called to forsake that lifeless form, leaving it, like a deserted palace, beautiful in its desolation. The hair dripping with the salt wave, curled in glossy abundance on the finely-formed head; the flat, broad brow; the closed eye, with its long black lashes; the firm, manly mouth; the strongly-moulded chin,—all, all were sealed with that seal which is never to be broken until the great resurrection day.

He was lying in a full suit of broadcloth, with a white vest and smart blue neck-tie, fastened with a pin, in which was some braided hair under a crystal. All his clothing was saturated with sea-water, which trickled from time to time, and struck with a leaden and dropping sound into a sullen pool which lay under the table.

Now comes the roll of wheels, and the Doctor's gig drives up to the door; and, as he goes creaking up with his heavy boots, we will follow and gain admission to the dimly-lighted chamber.

Two gossips are sitting in earnest, whispering conversation over a small bundle done up in an old flannel petticoat. To them the doctor is about to address himself cheerily, but is repelled by sundry signs and sounds which warn him not to speak. Moderating his heavy boots as well as he is able to a pace of quiet, he advances for a moment, and the petticoat is unfolded for him to glance at its contents; while a low, eager, whispered conversation, attended with much head-shaking, warns him that his first duty is with somebody behind the checked curtains of a bed in the farther corner of the room. He steps on tiptoe, and draws the curtain; and there, with closed eye, and cheek as white as the wintry snow, lies the same face over which passed the shadow of death when the ill-fated ship went down.

This woman was wife to him who lies below, and within the hour has been made mother to a frail little human existence, which on the storm of a great anguish has driven untimely on the shores of life,—a precious pearl cast up from the past eternity upon the wet, wave-ribbed sand of the present. Now weary with her moanings, and beaten out with the wrench of a double anguish, she lies with closed eyes in that passive apathy which precedes deeper shadows and longer rest.

Over against her, sits an aged woman in an attitude of deep dejection, and the old man we saw with her in the morning is standing with an anxious, awestruck face at the foot of the bed.

The doctor feels the pulse of the woman, or rather lays an inquiring finger where the slightest thread of vital current is barely throbbing, and shakes his head mournfully.

The touch of his hand rouses her,—her large wild, melancholy eyes fix themselves on him with an inquiring glance, then she shivers and moans,—

"Oh, Doctor, Doctor!—Jamie, Jamie!"

"Come, come!" said the doctor, "cheer up, my girl, you've got a fine little daughter,—the Lord mingles mercies with his afflictions."

Her eyes closed, her head moved with a mournful but decided dissent.

A moment after she spoke in the sad old words of the Hebrew Scripture,—

"Call her not Naomi; call her Mara, for the Almighty hath dealt very bitterly with me."

And as she spoke, there passed over her face the sharp frost of the last winter; but even as it passed there broke out a smile, as if a flower had been thrown from Paradise, and she said,—

"Not my will, but thy will," and so was gone.

The story of the wreck of the *Hanover* and how it affected a household on Orr's Island was first conceived by Harriet Beecher Stowe in the year 1852, three years after the disaster, but it was not until 1860 that she took up the tale in earnest.

Across at Pond Island Lighthouse lived young Milton Spinney, son of the keeper. Writing years later, he tells of the wreck of the craft launched in Bath, Maine, in 1838, and wrecked on November 9, 1849, on Pond Island Bar. I quote excerpts from his story.

The *Hanover* had sailed away in spring for a Russian port on the Black Sea where she had discharged her cargo, from there she sailed to Cadiz where she loaded salt for Bath, and was on her way home.

Without anything unusual happening to her she would be due at the mouth of the Kennebec River about the first of November. As the time drew near for her to appear off

the coast many pairs of eyes scanned the sea for a sight of
the ship. It had been blowing a number of days with the
wind east-north-east and it had created a heavy sea on the
coast.

I was ashore with one of our neighbor boys and it was
so rough that I could not get back to the island. I think
it was on the fourth day of the blow that in the morning
we saw Captain Rogers in the *Hanover* lying to the eastward of Seguin, which lies three miles off Pond Island.

There are two entrances to the Kennebec, one to the
eastward and one to the westward of Seguin. Captain
Rogers was considered a good pilot and fisherman and
pilots on the shore wondered why he did not run into the
river which he could easily have done with almost a fair
wind by coming in the western way.

When it was seen by the men on shore what Captain
Rogers intended to do they ran for a little hill that over-
looked the beach and farther out the breaking on a bar.
Behind them came the women and children, myself with
the rest.

The ship, when she headed up, although close hauled by
the wind, would have weathered the bar and Pond Island
if the tide had been running in, but just after she got by the
point of the treacherous sand spit she met the tide coming
out which caught her on the weather bow making impossible the ship's passing the island on that tack.

Taking the western way was one of the many unexplain-
able things connected with this tragedy. After lying all the
forenoon in a position where he could easily have entered
the river, in the afternoon Captain Rogers was seen to
square away his yards, run down to leeward of Seguin and
try to get in the western way.

Then we saw from our lookout that the Captain was
going to put his ship about. Slowly the vessel came up to

the wind, but a short distance from the seething foam of the bar and dead to windward of it.

When in the wind's eye she refused to go farther and with all her sails aback she slowly forged astern. Back, back, until every watcher's heart was ready to burst with suspense, back to that fearful maelstrom. Back, to the octopus whose arms were extended to receive the doomed ship and her crew. Back, till in the hollow of a huge wave her stempost struck the sand beneath and the story is told.

The ship, when she struck, fell off broadside to the sea and the next comber rolled her down on her broadside, then every man on board, twenty-four all told, were seen on her side. The next waves rolled her bottom-up, breaking her spars off. As she rolled over the crew clambered up over the bilge and strung themselves out, holding on to the keel.

The third and fourth seas broke the ship in pieces and left the crew to battle for their lives till death should end their troubles. We knew that no man could come through alive.

As the wreckage came floating ashore the men went on the beach, and as the bodies came ashore they were reverently carried up on the high ground and laid down. Before the end of the day the bodies had been secured and now lie buried in a little cemetery within sound of the roaring waves which beat them to death.

There was never a real memorial or gravestone erected at the Percy Burial Ground, near Cox's Head, where most of the remains are interred.

6

The *Dash*

Various parts of the New England coast are noted for legendary craft. Block Island, Rhode Island, has the *Princess Augusta*, said to appear on warm nights in the summer, identified by the glow of her burning in the sky. Actually, the *Princess Augusta* never did burn, but the legend has continued since the year 1738, when she sank at the end of a long voyage from Europe, during which more than a hundred Palatine passengers lost their lives.

In my *Legends of the New England Coast*, which I wrote in 1957, there is a chapter on such phantom ships. Since that time I have had letter after letter asking for more details on one of the phantom craft included, the *Dash*, which was launched in Portland in 1812.

No craft was superior to the *Dash* in speed until the days of the clipper ships. The best ships of the British Navy chased her for months, but she was never captured. She maintained her position upon the sea through the War of 1812, taking valuable prizes. Finally she succumbed to the element upon which she had won her triumphs, going down at the height of a winter's gale.

The record of this vessel, as papers from her successful voyages remain to show, was one that even conjecture has not improved. The *Ariel* of novelist Cooper was not the equal of this Maine craft.

Even in her conception the *Dash* was unique. In the early 1800's the drafting of plans for a vessel was practically unknown, and the solid model was undreamed of. The prevailing practice was simply to lay a keel, set up at either end a stem and stern post, and fill in between the frames, shaping the hull "by the eye" as the work progressed.

Of course, the results of this sort of building were not always satisfactory, the two sides of the vessel being seldom the same shape, so a craft would frequently sail faster on one tack than she would on the other.

However, the builders of the *Dash* wanted a craft that could show the highest type of speed. They realized that in the service for which she was designed, such a vessel must be either a flyer or a failure. Being experienced shipwrights as well as shipowners, they were able to call on practical knowledge in the solution of this problem, and the first ship's model that the state of Maine ever knew was the result. Of course, it was unlike the solid models that came afterward. Upon a backboard, pieces of wood to represent halves of frames were nailed, thin layers of wood were tacked upon them, and thus the skeleton of one half of a vessel was made. By repeated trimmings and cuttings, the lines of the hull were perfected until what seemed to be the required shape for speed had been secured, after which the keel was laid.

The men who constructed this craft were John and Seward Porter of Portland, and the vessel was built in their yard at Porter's Landing, their old home.

Barely a few rotten piles of the wharf from which the *Dash* was launched now remain. The yard where so many fine vessels were built has long since been overrun by grass, but the model of the *Dash* has been preserved carefully as an heirloom. Indeed, it was one of the most interesting relics brought to light during the work of collecting Maine's exhibit for the 1893 World's Fair.

The model is especially interesting to marine architects of today because it is an unanswerable refutation of the claim, so often made, that the sharp floor lines of the modern yacht did not exist until the 1890's. Except for its almost perpendicular sternpost, the model might easily represent a craft of the Burgess class, since the bow is sharp, the run begins amidships, and all the floor timbers are at a sharp angle. All the lines are very suggestive of the world-renowned Boston clippers of the 1850's.

The *Dash* was not, however, originally designed to be a privateer; she was merely a natural product of the times. For years both English and French vessels had been troubling the Americans, and when the embargo was ordered, no ordinary craft could venture to sea with any prospect of success. Therefore ships lay dismantled at the wharves or swung idly in harbors, warehouses went uncared for, and the merchant marine of the United States was literally paralyzed. Then it was that some venturesome men possessed themselves of fast, speedy craft. Defying danger, they made immense profits out of risky voyages, since West Indian products sold at exorbitant prices. Therefore, when war was formally declared, the Porters built this vessel to run the gauntlet of English warships between Cuba and Portland, much as the blockade-runners operated during the Civil War.

Historian Edward Clarence Plummer wrote more than eighty years ago of the risks these vessels ran at that time. He emphasized that the danger could be better appreciated when it is remembered that the United States was then practically without a navy. Only five of our craft could be rightly claimed as fighting ships, while England had almost ninety vessels regularly cruising in Maine waters. During the War of 1812 Great Britain sometimes showed more than one hundred sail in the

North Atlantic. Nevertheless, the superiority of American ships over those of foreign build, combined with the unequaled skill of American sailors, had even then been demonstrated. Yankee confidence was fully equal to the emergency.

The *Dash* was rigged as a topsail schooner—a favorite style in those days. Her home port was Portland, and there she was fitted for the sea. She first sailed unobserved to Santo Domingo and disposed of a cargo at good prices. Then, loaded with coffee, the *Dash* was well on her way home when she was sighted by a British man-of-war, which sent a cannonball invitation for her to come about and "await the pleasure of His Majesty's representative."

Captain Kelleran, however, an officer well known in his day, was in command, and he would not entertain the idea of losing his handsome vessel on her maiden trip. He simply piled on the canvas, pitched overboard enough of his cargo to let his little schooner take advantage of her racing form, and permitted the Englishman to fade slowly away in the distance. It was a narrow escape, as the foremast was badly sprung and nearly taken out of the *Dash* by the strain.

The *Dash* returned to Portland safely, having proved herself an excellent sailer. But her master had noticed that if her sail plan were altered she could be made to give an even better account of herself. The split foremast was removed, a heavier spar put in its place, and square sails added, making the *Dash* a hermaphrodite brig. A tremendous spread of light sails was given her, and then, like many of the later Gloucester fishermen, she was ready to tackle anything that came her way.

One of the disadvantages under which the *Dash* labored, as did most American vessels of those days, was lack of sheathing, copper being very costly. Thus the unprotected bottom became foul very quickly, while the British cruisers, sheathed in metal, were always in racing trim. The Yankee captain avoided this handicap, in a measure, by giving his craft a coating of tallow and soap just before starting out on a voyage. Although this mixture soon wore away, it was good while it lasted. Incidentally, both tallow and soap were cheap in this period of our nation's economy.

The *Dash* started out again, with improved chances of success. British war vessels began a chase almost at once, the largest of them no less than a seventy-four-gun ship. The *Dash* sailed away as usual and landed her cargo in good order, but at the height of one of the races she had to sacrifice her two bow guns and part of her deck load to get into necessary trim. The fact that coffee was then selling at a dollar a pound made the profits from this voyage highly satisfactory.

So far the missions of the *Dash* had been peaceful. All her captain asked was that she be left alone. But now came the days when the Americans stood up to the English on the high seas. The fighting fever was upon the people, and because of this a new captain was appointed to the *Dash*. A new feeling of confidence developed in New England, and it was agreed that taking cargo was easier than purchasing it in foreign ports. The *Dash* was now fitted out as a first-class privateer, with the guns for such a bold venture on board.

The small broadside cannon which the *Dash* had been carrying for her own protection were removed, and two eighteen-pounders were taken instead. The "long Tom" or "thirty-two" that had been mounted amidships was retained.

A larger crew was needed and shipped, and the *Dash* started out, not exactly looking for trouble, but with the purpose of doing less running in the future. The captain vowed that he would take charge of the first British merchantman sighted.

Unfortunately, the *Dash* ran into a giant British seventy-four-gun man-of-war. The seventy-four was not the kind of game she was seeking, and the *Dash* fled under full sail, quickly dropping the man-of-war below the horizon. Shortly afterward she was approached by a cruiser only slightly larger than her own size, showed fight, won a victory, and carried a valuable cargo to port.

Then came a spectacular record of prizes. Encountering the armed ship *Lacedemonian*, she captured her, together with the American sloop which the British ship was carrying off in triumph. A little later the *Dash* was chased by a frigate and a schooner. She outsailed the frigate, drew the schooner away from the protection of the big ship, whipped her soundly, and went on her way.

Her captain at this time was a young man whose merits President Lincoln years later recognized by making him customs inspector at Portland. Captain William Cammett, an outstanding sailor, according to Edward Clarence Plummer, was a man who never saw the Union Jack without having a desire to fight.

The *Dash* continued her successful career, taking cargoes from English vessels when she could find them, buying them in port when she could not, and capturing many prizes in addition. She had made herself a terror to the British merchant marine. The *Dash* was the pride of Portland and all Casco Bay, but the object of a most emphatic hatred on the part of the British man-of-war's sailor, who could "no more catch her than he could corner the will-o'-the-wisp."

Finally the *Dash* was put under the command of Captain John Porter, a young brother of the owners, then only twenty-four years of age, but a youth who had already established a fine record. He made two captures within a week of leaving port. Then he retook the American privateer *Armistice*, which had just fallen to the English frigate *Pactolus*, and a few days later added two brigs and a sloop to the list. When Captain Porter came back to port to refit, after being absent less than three months, he had already sent home six prizes.

Under Porter's command, the *Dash* reached the zenith of her glory. She could show a record unsurpassed by any other

American privateer. She had never known defeat, had never attacked a vessel in vain, had never been injured by an enemy shot, and it was claimed that her equal in speed did not exist. Thus it was that young men came to compete for the privilege of signing on as members of her crew.

It was considered a high honor to be pointed out as belonging to the *Dash*, for it was the equivalent of saying that a man or youth had made the grade. Men from families in Portland and almost every surrounding town were in her crew, and every family sending a representative aboard the *Dash* was proud of the honor.

Her history was a glorious one when she started on her last and fatal cruise. It was the middle of January, 1815. Unconscious of the fact that a treaty of peace between the United States and Great Britain had already been signed, the crew of the *Dash* were impatient to be away after more glory and more prize money. The canvas was crowded upon the tall, tapering masts. Ready for sea, the rakish craft sailed up and down the harbor waiting for the coming of the captain, who alone of the ship's company was not on board.

Meanwhile their commander was bidding farewell to his young wife. Married but a few months, the happy couple seemed to know by instinct that they should not part and that this would be their last meeting. The signal gun had sounded over Casco Bay for him, but still Captain Porter did not heed its summons. Lingering until a second gun told him that he must obey the call, Porter then hurried away to the landing.

What little is known of the fate of the *Dash* is told by the crew of the *Champlain*, a new privateer that waited in the harbor to try her speed against that of the Portland champion on an outward cruise.

Leaving the harbor together, the two ships took a southerly course. The *Dash* drew away to the front, and at the close of the next day was far in the lead. Then a gale came on, and the *Dash* was last seen shooting away into driving clouds of snow that soon hid her from sight. The master of the *Champlain*, fearing Georges Shoals, altered his course and came out of the gale in safety. Nothing more was ever heard of the *Dash*.

Probably Captain Porter, with the crude instruments of those days, failed to estimate his speed correctly and was on the shoals before he suspected his danger. All who have seen the miles of breakers hurrying over these "rapids of the sea" can understand why sailors fear them so. It is certainly possible that the *Dash* foundered there.

For months, even years, those whose loved ones had gone out aboard the *Dash* refused to believe them lost. Year followed year, however, with never a word of hope. The steps of those who for so many long months had climbed to the high observatory on Munjoy's Hill to ask if any news had come grew less frequent upon the stair. The thought that some time at least one of the crew would come back to tell the vessel's fate was gradually forgotten, and mothers came to know their sons were dead.

Not a single piece of wreckage ever reached the shore. No floating spar or splintered boat ever appeared to offer its mute testimony. The vessel disappeared as completely as if she had been one of her own cannonballs dropped into the sea. Only her model and the records of her successful voyages remain.

Bror Tamm of Quincy, Massachusetts, a well-known naval architect who made a complete study of all the known facts concerning the *Dash*, says of her fate, "All indications are that she capsized. Hell-bent for speed, she had a big crew and probably went right over on her beam ends."

In the year 1866 John Greenleaf Whittier wrote what is possibly the best-known poem regarding phantom vessels. It was called "The Dead Ship of Harpswell" and was based on the loss of the *Dash*.

A letter of Whittier's,* written at Oak Knoll, Danvers, Massachusetts, in 1889, tells how he composed the poem:

*The letter is now in the Hollingsworth Collection at St. Paul's School, Concord, New Hampshire.

My dear Friend:

Some 25 years ago I received from Miss Marion Pearl, daughter of the Rev. Mr. Pearl, a well-known clergyman of Maine, a letter descriptive of the people, dialects, customs, superstitions, and legends of Orr's Island where, I think, the writer was a teacher. The legend of a spectre ship, as described in my poem, attracted me by its weird suggestiveness. Miss Pearl is now, I believe, the wife of an officer in the U.S. Army. I think I had a second letter from her confirming the story, but I fail to find it among my papers. I have no doubt that a quarter of a century ago the legend was talked of on the island, by the aged people. It was I am sure no invention of Miss Pearl. Perhaps it has died out now. The schoolmaster has been abroad since, and the new generation are ashamed of the fireside lore of their grandmothers.

I am glad thee are working in the line of these old stories. We need them all in this matter of fact age.

I am truly thy friend
John G. Whittier

It is true that the legend was "no invention" of Miss Pearl. The craft in question was the *Dash*, a topsail schooner of 222 tons, launched in 1812.

Whittier's poem appears below, together with the introductory stanza he wrote acknowledging its source.

Introductory Stanza
Shifting his scattered papers, 'Here,'
He said, as died the faint applause,
'Is something that I found last year
Down on the island known as Orr's.
I had it from a fair-haired girl
Who, oddly, bore the name of Pearl,

(As if by some droll freak of circumstance,)
Classic, or wellnigh so, in Harriet Stowe's
   romance.'

The Dead Ship of Harpswell

What flecks the outer gray beyond
   The sundown's golden trail?
The white flash of a sea-bird's wing,
   Or gleam of slanting sail?
Let young eyes watch from Neck and Point,
   And sea-worn elders pray,—
The ghost of what was once a ship
   Is sailing up the bay!

From gray sea-fog, from icy drift,
   From peril and from pain,
The home-bound fisher greets thy lights,
   O hundred-harbored Maine!
But many a keel shall seaward turn,
   And many a sail outstand,
When, tall and white, the Dead Ship looms
   Against the dusk of land.

She rounds the headland's bristling pines;
   She threads the isle-set bay;
No spur of breeze can speed her on,
   Nor ebb of tide delay.
Old men still walk the Isle of Orr
   Who tell her date and name,
Old shipwrights sit in Freeport yards
   Who hewed her oaken frame.

What weary doom of baffled quest,
   Thou sad sea-ghost, is thine?
What makes thee in the haunts of home

A wonder and a sign?
No foot is on thy silent deck,
    Upon thy helm no hand;
No ripple hath the soundless wind
    That smites thee from the land!

For never comes the ship to port,
    Howe'er the breeze may be;
Just when she nears the waiting shore
    She drifts again to sea.
No tack of sail, nor turn of helm,
    Nor sheer of veering side;
Stern-fore she drives to sea and night,
    Against the wind and tide.

In vain o'er Harpswell Neck the star
    Of evening guides her in;
In vain for her the lamps are lit
    Within thy tower, Seguin!
In vain the harbor-boat shall hail,
    In vain the pilot call;
No hand shall reef her spectral sail,
    Or let her anchor fall.

Shake, brown old wives, with dreary joy,
    Your gray-head hints of ill;
And, over sick-beds whispering low,
    Your prophecies fulfil.
Some home amid yon birchen trees
    Shall drape its door with woe;
And slowly where the Dead Ship sails,
    The burial boat shall row!

From Wolf Neck and from Flying Point,
    From island and from main,

From sheltered cove and tided creek,
    Shall glide the funeral train.
The dead-boat with the bearers four,
    The mourners at her stern,—
And one shall go the silent way
    Who shall no more return!

And men shall sigh, and women weep,
    Whose dear ones pale and pine,
And sadly over sunset seas
    Await the ghostly sign.
They know not that its sails are filled
    By pity's tender breath
Nor see the Angel at the helm
    Who steers the Ship of Death!

William Hutchinson Rowe quotes a poem on the same theme,
which he found in a newspaper, possibly around 1900:

You have heard of the ship that sails the bay,
    With night for helmsman and death in tow,
And that glides to sea as he comes ashore
    And speeds on his errand of woe.

It was in the year of Eighteen-Twelve
    They launched the *Dash* from a Freeport yard,
She sails the bay as the 'Dead Ship' now,
    You have heard her doom from the Quaker bard.

She was manned by a crew of gallant lads
    As ever a vessel's deck had trod,
A score and a hundred of them all—
    And their fate is known to none but God.

They all belonged to the towns around,

There were brothers and cousins and comrades too,
Full armed and equipped they put to sea,
    And the skies were never a softer blue.

But weeks and months and years sped on,
    And hearts grew hopeless and cheeks grew pale,
And eyes are dim that have watched so long
    To catch a glimpse of her home bound sail.

But when any of those who loved the lads
    Are ready to slip their moorings here
And sail away to the unknown port
    You will see the Dead Ship gliding near.

And the ship and the life go out with the tide,
    And the captain paused for awhile, then said
'They are most all gone and the Dead Ship soon
    Will come no more for the souls of the dead!'

7

The Loss of the *Bohemian*

Some shipwrecks seem destined, while others are apparently pure bad luck.

The loss of life aboard the Allen Line steamer *Bohemian* can be blamed at least in part on bad luck, because it occurred on the evening of a holiday celebration.

The *Bohemian*, built by W. Denny and Brothers, was capable of a speed of thirteen knots and was 298 feet long. Her direct-acting engines were the best of the time.

The *Bohemian* sailed from Liverpool on February 4, 1864, with a passenger list of 218 and a crew of 99. Captain Borland made a brief stop at Londonderry before starting out across the ocean. Stormy weather delayed the vessel several days, and so it was late on the afternoon of February 22 when the *Bohemian* made Cape Elizabeth, Maine.

A peculiar condition of haze confused Captain Borland into believing that he was quite a distance off the shores of Cape Elizabeth, although actually he was approaching Alden's Rock, about halfway between Hue and Cry Ledge and Cape Elizabeth Lights. Realizing that he needed help, he sent up rockets and blue lights to attract the attention of a pilot, at the same time slowing his speed to a knot and a half. He also ordered the firing of the ship's gun, hoping someone would assist him.

Suddenly, without warning, the *Bohemian* crashed against Alden's Rock and slid over. A hasty examination revealed a bad leak in the engine compartment, so the captain headed the *Bohemian* for land, at the same time ordering all lifeboats over. The crew took their stations in orderly fashion, but the passengers became excited and milled around the boats in confusion. When the number-two lifeboat was loaded, the pin broke, dropping everyone into the sea.

The other lifeboats were successfully launched, although only partially filled with passengers. Captain Borland ordered the rowers to return to the ship, as there were more than eighty persons still aboard the vessel. They refused, heading at once for shore, where they all landed safely. Three hours later, however, others brought the lifeboats back to the *Bohemian*, and the remaining survivors were taken ashore without accident.

The fact that it was Washington's birthday caused an unfortunate interpretation of the ship's distress rockets and the firing of the ship's gun. Several pilots had heard the cannon's firing and had seen the rockets in the air, but concluded that some patriotic festivities were being celebrated in honor of George Washington. They gave the matter no further thought.

Later Captain Borland testified that the peculiar haze made the land look many miles farther away than was actually the case. He was being cautious and had two lookouts on the forecastle and one aloft. Although he attempted to reach land, the *Bohemian* went down in four fathoms in an upright position so that her upper works were above the surface of the sea.

Twenty Irish immigrants had been drowned when the number-two lifeboat capsized on launching, but no others were lost. The weather, although foggy, was mild and calm, with a heavy ground swell. It is believed that if the *Bohemian* could have remained afloat another minute, she would have safely reached shore.*

There was a good deal of mail aboard the steamer, and divers were sent down later to recover it. Although Charles Hocking in his excellent two-volume work, *Disasters at Sea*, tells us that all the mail was recovered, this is not quite so, as mail for Philadelphia was never brought to the surface.

Tradition, often incorrect, tells us that John F. Fitzgerald, famous Boston mayor and grandfather of John F. Kennedy, was aboard the *Bohemian* when she was wrecked. When I asked Mr. Fitzgerald about the details, he explained that it was another John Fitzgerald who was aboard the unfortunate craft on that Washington's birthday in 1864.

*Robert Thayer Sterling, in his scholarly *Lighthouses of the Maine Coast*, gives a fine account of the wreck of the *Bohemian*.

8

The *Oakey L. Alexander*

On March 3, 1947, the area around Cape Elizabeth was swept by a gale unequaled in the memory of the oldest inhabitant. Foundering in the terrible storm at a point near the Portland Lightship was the coal collier *Oakey L. Alexander*. This 395-foot steamer had made over eight hundred successful trips from the south to Portland. Her master, Captain Raymond Lewis, was in the wheelhouse. Standing at his side was First Mate John G. Walker of Norfolk, Virginia. At the wheel was Quartermaster Clifford Watts. All three knew that the *Alexander* was in a very dangerous position. Not only was the barometer reading lower than it had been in either the great Portland Gale or the hurricane that hit in 1938, but the wind was blowing more fiercely than at any other time in the local weather bureau's history, sixty-three miles an hour with gusts as high as eighty.

The officers on the bridge of the *Alexander* soon detected the white, flashing gleam of *Portland Lightship* and laid their course accordingly. But what they could not know was that the lightship had been pulled from her moorings by the great storm and was even then several miles off station. The gale had driven her into a section of the outer bay where the crashing breakers were twenty-five and thirty feet high.

Repeatedly, towering billows with breaking crests smashed against the *Alexander*. Repeatedly the *Alexander* shook herself free. The vibrations on board indicated that almost half the time the propeller was out of water. The storm was completely overwhelming the collier. The relentless power of thirty-foot waves can do terrible things to a ship.

Suddenly, at 4:20 A.M., it happened. A terrific forty-foot wave enveloped the *Alexander* as she neared the lightship. With her stern in the trough of the sea and her amidships section deep in the wave, her bow was thrust forward well out of water, momentarily suspended in midair ahead of the giant breaker.

The seconds passed, and still the 395-foot collier rode the breaker, but the strain was too great for the structure to endure. A moment later, with a terrific wrenching, grinding, and ripping, the bow of the unlucky ship split off and vanished before the three startled men on the bridge.

Captain Lewis, Mate Walker, and Quartermaster Watts could not believe their eyes, but they knew it must have happened. One hundred and thirty-five feet of their ship had disappeared as they watched, and they were sure the portion on which they stood was about to plunge into the sea and take them all to death. Thirty-two men were to be sacrificed to the god of storm.

But the moments passed, and the ship did not go down! Could it be that the bulkheads were still watertight amidships and aft? It seemed a forlorn hope, but it was possible.

A brief conference was held. It was found that the *Alexander* had broken in two just forward of the number-four hatch. Despite this, the bulkheads were holding, and most remarkable of all, the engine room was dry. With a prayer of thankfulness, Captain Lewis ordered all men to stand by. He was proud of his crew, who were calm and determined.

"Men," he said, "I think we still have a good chance if we can keep steam up. If you can work the automatic stokers, we'll make it. It's our only hope. Now, back to your posts, all of you. I'll call you three minutes before I think she'll hit."

Engineer Winfield S. Brower glanced at his two assistants, Arthur Bradley and William Simpson. It was up to them, and they realized it. They were going back to their posts in the engine room, where they would be the first to die should the ship strike unexpectedly. The three men returned to their stations, where they remained for more than an hour working the automatic stokers.

Up on the bridge, Captain Lewis and Chief Officer Walker were joined by Second Mate Floyd Light and Third Mate George H. Stewart. They took turns blowing the five blasts of distress at regular intervals, and each man prayed that the whistles were being heard ashore above the roar of the storm and the boom of the breakers. To the men on the bridge, the sound of the whistle was deafening. When they stepped outside, the tempest whipped through their coats, and they braced themselves against the vessel's pitch and toss. The gigantic waves were slowly taking them toward land.

Suddenly there was a shout!

"There's a light, Captain, two points off the starboard bow!" Every eye peered into the darkness. Sure enough, there was a gleam of light and then darkness again—a long interval of darkness. They all knew that if it were Cape Elizabeth Lights, there would be six flashes in sequence. Then it came again, and all began to count:

One-two-three-four-five-six. Yes, it was Cape Elizabeth, and they would soon know their fate. Captain Lewis ordered the engines slowed so that when they hit, the shock would not be too great. Within a short time, through the early morning gloom, he sighted the ledges and cliffs of Cape Elizabeth itself and ordered every one up on deck. The three engineers ran for the ladder, and two minutes later had made their way to the bridge.

Captain Lewis maneuvered the broken half of his vessel to a suitable position just off Crescent Beach, but the most difficult task was ahead. Could he beach the bowless collier on the hard, ironlike ledges?

"All hands stand ready!" he roared. "I'm taking her in."

"Here we go!" shouted several of the crew, and with a rumbling, bumping, thundering crash, the iron ship hit the shore's rocky shelf and slid along. Higher and higher the *Alexander* went, for Captain Lewis steered his course well. Then, with a final grinding crunch, the collier came to a complete stop just two hundred yards from the wave-washed, grass-covered cliffs of McKenny's Point at Cape Elizabeth.

Captain Lewis murmured a grateful prayer and walked out on the flying bridge. There was no one in sight onshore, but soon he detected a group coming over the hillside. The men of the coast guard were on the way.

Back at the Cape Elizabeth Station, some minutes before the *Alexander* grounded, Boatswain Robbins was strangely uneasy. Was that the whistle of a ship in distress? He went outside to learn if he could hear it again. The sound was unmistakable, several short blasts from a steamer evidently right offshore. A vessel was in trouble; there could be no doubt about it. Robbins notified the officer in command, Chief Warrant Boatswain Earle B. Drinkwater, and the chief ordered the rescue gear made ready. It was a period of economy in the coast guard service, however, and only four men could be spared. The normal crew of eleven had been cut to less than half! Soon several old-time coastguardsmen, grizzled veterans of countless rescues, joined the group, and later a number of local fishermen appeared.

The whistle from the ship in distress kept sounding, and the men followed its blast until they reached Crescent Beach and McKenny's Point. There they found the *Alexander*, on the ledges below them, each wave pounding the stern of the vessel and sweeping across her deck. Rushing their apparatus to the edge of a cliff near the ship, Chief Drinkwater made sure that all was in readiness for the firing of the Lyle gun. Setting it at the proper angle and allowing for the wind, he loaded it with the eighteen-pound shot. Shaped like a three-inch shell, the shot had a spindle and an eye on the end. Helped by the others, Drinkwater took the faking box, which holds hundreds of feet of strong linen cord, and rubbed several feet of the line into the mud so that when the gun was fired the flash would not burn the line. Then he carefully tied it to the eye on the end of the shot.

"Everyone stand back!" he shouted. The coastguardsman aimed at the wrecked vessel two hundred yards away and fired. It was the first time he had ever shot a Lyle gun. Drinkwater was gratified to see the line reach its mark and watched the sailors on the flying bridge of the *Alexander* make it fast. Then Drinkwater attached to the line a pulley, known as a tail block, and an endless rope called a whip. When all was ready, he signaled to the men on the wreck that they should pull away.

Out on the ship the crew pulled with a will. The tail block and the whip reached the *Alexander*, and they too were made fast. Then the heavy three-inch hawser was sent out and secured at a point two feet above the ship. On shore Drinkwater ordered the breeches buoy itself attached to the whip's endless line. The breeches buoy is really a canvas seat with two openings for the legs to go through. A ring resembling a life preserver goes completely around the top of the canvas seat, and the ring is secured to the traveling block on the hawser by four strong lines.

All present watched the breeches buoy make its journey out to the *Alexander*. Each man knew he was in extreme danger until the moment he landed safely on the opposite cliff. Each remembered many cases where the breeches buoy had jammed with a sailor caught under the waves and drowned before he could be rescued.

"Who wants to try it first?" called out Captain Lewis.

"I do, sir," shouted messboy David Rogers, the youngest member of the crew, and he climbed into the canvas seat and pushed his legs through the openings. It was 8:02 A.M. A moment later he was speeding ashore. Within five minutes he had landed on the cliffs of Cape Elizabeth, the first person ashore that morning from the broken collier.

"All hands are safe," the messboy informed the excited group gathered about him. The breeches buoy had already been sent back to the ship for the next passenger. Again and again the trip was accomplished successfully. When Radio Operator Lorenz Connolly of Boston was part way to shore, however, the lines jammed briefly and poor Connolly was under the waves for about twenty seconds. Two others were submerged on their journey ashore, but Connolly had suffered the most and was rushed to the hospital.

Finally, the time came when only two officers remained aboard the broken collier. The empty breeches buoy arrived at the flying bridge, and Captain Lewis placed his hand on the other's shoulder. "You are next; go ahead now. I'll stay with her just a little longer." Five minutes later Mate Walker had landed on the windy bluff, safe and sound. Then the breeches buoy was sent out for the last time.

Captain Raymond Lewis, who had accomplished a feat that would be talked about for years to come, glanced briefly around at what was left of the *Alexander*. It was the last time he would be aboard her as commander. He thought of the hundreds of successful voyages he and his ship had taken together, and then, with a half sob, he stepped into the breeches buoy and was hauled ashore. Nearing the bluff, Captain Lewis was greeted by shouts of encouragement. He landed safely on the edge of the cliff a moment later. Because of his determination and sagacity not a single life had been lost.

I had flown up from Boston to reach the scene of the disaster that morning, and I talked with Chief Drinkwater of the United States Coast Guard. We walked over to the cottage where the crew members were resting, and as I came in I heard one of the sailors talking:

"I've said some pretty tough things about the coast guard in my day, but from now on I'm all for 'em." And that's the way every one of the thirty-two rescued men from the *Alexander* felt.

Later that week Captain John G. Snow of Rockland and I stood with Drinkwater at the scene of the wreck. "Chief," I began, "is there anything you'd like to go on record about, anything you'd like to have mentioned?"

"Why, yes," he replied, somewhat surprised. "That's a good idea. It would be fine if you'd mention my men: Robbins, Taylor, Spaulding, Doucette, Brown, and Morong, and the men from the South Portland Base. They did a magnificent job of it all the way through. Then there were the fishermen, and the retired coast guardsmen, who came when they were needed. You should name Roscoe Dennison, Verne Reynolds, and Melcher Beal. They deserve the praise of everyone who hears about it. I'd like to thank them all."

For the first time in the history of Casco Bay, notes and documents written on board a vessel at the moment of extreme danger are available to the reader. I have received from the master of the *Oakey L. Alexander*, Captain Raymond W. Lewis, vital material which he wrote at the time of the disaster:

4 A.M., 135 feet off bow forward of No. 4, six miles off Portland. Sea came from aft before could clear and another

came and broke her in two. Port side hung on for a while, slipped back and forth, and then broke. In company with lightship.

Snowing horribly, listed 15°, lost both lifeboats, one drifted away, other smashed in davits. Daylight came just in time, made Anthony bell buoy. All men out of engine room but chief engineer and asst. Master kept calling down to engine room.

Every member of the crew was taken ashore by breeches buoy, the first going at 8:02 that morning and the last, Captain Raymond William Lewis, at 10:55, not quite three hours later. The coast guard praised Captain Lewis later in a special commendation awarded to him. The master of the *Alexander* was cited for his outstanding work in helping to bring all of his crew ashore alive.

9

The *Don* Mystery

A strange Casco Bay mystery was the loss, with all persons aboard, of the forty-four-foot cabin cruiser *Don*, which disappeared at sea on June 29, 1941. A trip from Dyer's Cove, East Harpswell, Maine, to Monhegan Island had been planned by Albert Melanson of Rumford as an outing for residents who lived in Rumford and Mexico, Maine, two towns close to each other, and situated some eighty miles north of Portland.

The thirty-four excursionists were to board the *Don* at about seven o'clock Sunday morning, June 29. However, the various delays that almost always occur in setting forth on such expeditions postponed the departure until nine thirty.

With all his party on board, Captain Paul Johnson steered the *Don* out through the channel, landing later at West Point near Cape Small. There the passengers went ashore at Reed's General Store, where some of them addressed postcards to the loved ones they were fated never to see again. Miss Beatrice Roach mailed a card to her mother which read, "Feeling fine, not seasick. But there is still 30 more miles to go, Bea."

At eleven o'clock that morning the *Don* headed for sea again; this time her destination was Monhegan Island. According to those who watched her departure, the fog that had been threatening all morning was thickening just a trifle as the *Don* disappeared down the bay.

As darkness fell there was no word of any sort from the excursionists who had left Dyer's Cove in such a happy mood. Relatives and friends became concerned, especially as the fog was getting denser. Midnight passed, but attempts of other craft to search for the *Don* were hampered by the lack of visibility, limiting the area in which the rescuers could cruise.

The Damariscove Island Coast Guard was alerted, and for ten hours without rest a patrol boat searched through the foggy waters of Casco Bay for some sign of the missing cruiser. In charge of the operation was Captain Milton H. Seavy, who had as his assistants during the long, tiring marine vigil Thomas M. Manchester and John W. Foss.

The hours went by, and there were no new developments. When dawn broke Monday morning it was still foggy. A telephone call to Monhegan confirmed the fear that the *Don* had never reached her destination. Soon afterward a complete check of all locations revealed that she was not at any harbor or refuge in the area.

All that day the search went on, with many relatives and friends making their headquarters around the eleven empty cars the passengers had left at Dyer's Cove.

When the fog lifted briefly that Tuesday morning there was hope that the boat might be found drifting at sea with engine trouble, but again the hours passed without news of any sort.

Suddenly, all hopes were shattered when the bodies of two of the women passengers, Dorcas Kersey and Bessie Strople, were discovered floating in the sea off Bailey Island. A short time later another body was sighted, that of Anne Stisulis. The body of Elizabeth Howard was then found off Bailey Island. In all, fourteen bodies were eventually recovered.* Captain Paul

*Lobsterman Claude Johnson was instrumental in sighting and bringing in at least one of the victims.

Johnson's body was discovered attached to a wooden keg which was firmly tied to a rope around his waist. None of the victims wore a life preserver, indicating that whatever occurred took place suddenly. Several of the bodies were said to have been blackened and burned as if by an explosion, but this was later disputed.

As the days went by certain revelations concerning the *Don* were made. Residents who lived near Dyer's Cove stated that the boat had been allowed to stay in the ice at her moorings all the preceding winter. Others volunteered the information that she had gone to the bottom on two previous occasions when there had been no passengers aboard.

It was also claimed that Orrin Scott of the area had warned Captain Johnson two years before that the people of the vicinity would not consider Johnson one of themselves until he put some "good gear" on the *Don*, as she was then a "patch job."

The general theory was that gasoline in the bilge water exploded and fired the craft, and that the thick pea-soup fog lasting off and on until July 2 prevented more bodies from being discovered.

Two statements were given at the time, one by Paul C. Thurston, president of the Rumford Falls Trust Company, and the other by a prominent resident of the community, Douglas Fosdick. Thurston believed that the gas tank had been giving Captain Johnson trouble, as the latter had been working on it almost up to the time the trip started. He was of the opinion that the tank had developed a slight leak that morning, which produced fumes in the cabin and gasoline in the bilge. He believed that when Johnson lighted a fire to cook chowder, an explosion followed at once. Thurston did not believe that the boat had capsized. He was of the opinion that the tragedy occurred a little less than ten miles out to sea from West Point.

Douglas Fosdick stated that he believed Johnson had no license to operate a motorboat carrying passengers for hire. But in Fosdick's opinion the boat did not explode because of gasoline. He based his belief on the viewpoint of fishermen and medical examiners that the marks found on the bodies were bruises and not burns. "The hair on the skin of the victims was not burned off," Fosdick said.

The *Don* had been used as a rum-runner in prohibition days. She was a double-ender with a precariously high superstructure.

Clothing and watches found on the bodies of victims aided the searchers in getting some picture of what probably happened. A watch taken from the wrist of Marie Rose Coulombe was found stopped at 11:42, indicating the approximate time that fateful morning when the disaster occurred.

An editorial in the Rumford Falls *Times* of July 3, 1941, concluded that

the catastrophe that overtook the ill-fated party came with appalling suddenness. One moment they were chugging serenely along in the calm waters of Casco Bay. In another they were struggling for life in those dark waters. What heroic dramas were then enacted no man will ever know. Some perhaps died before they entered the water, some survived to swim briefly about the lost boat before their strength ebbed and failed.

On shore early Monday morning word was received that the boat was overdue, but efforts of searchers were hampered by the pea-soup thick fog banks that had rolled in covering the islands with a cottony blanket. Hope was sustained for twenty-four hours until Tuesday morning when the bodies of two women were found by a woman cottager.

Stunned by the magnitude of the calamity, Rumford and Mexico wait helplessly for the sea to give up the bodies of the souls it has claimed. All the honors that the living can extend to the dead will be ordered by the people of these communities. The pain of the loss is sharp. The grief is deep.

A day was set apart for memorial exercises for those who had lost their lives in the disaster. On Sunday, July 6, 1941, hundreds of people gathered at Rumford's Chisholm Park for services. To begin the memorial exercises appropriate music was played by the Rumford band, after which the opening remarks were given by Justice Albert Beliveau. He explained that "it was deemed fit by public-spirited citizens of the towns of Rumford and Mexico that such a demonstration as this should take place so that we might express in public our sorrow at the sudden departure of these well-known and prominent citizens, men and women of these two towns who, because of their work, came in contact daily with most of the people."

On the same day the memorial exercises were held at Rumford, other services were conducted at the church and at the wharf on Bailey Island. A sorrowful, impressive journey was made by the Sea and Shore Fisheries boat *Maine*. As she rounded the buoy off Mark Island Ledge, flowers were dropped from the boat into the sea. Onshore at the same moment, the Bailey Island flag was lowered to half-mast. Taps were sounded, and wreaths and flowers were thrown from the pier into the water. The Reverend James E. Herrick then offered a short prayer from the pier, and the Fisheries boat started back to the wharf. Because of the size of the church, services held inside the Bailey Island chapel could be attended by only a few of the hundreds of persons anxious to be present.

The years went by. In 1958 wreckage was found that might be that of the *Don*. I organized a search group to attempt positive identification of the hull, but the results of our underwater efforts did nothing to solve the mystery. Fifty-three letters concerning the disaster yielded much additional information I had not heard before. Whether that information is accurate is another matter.

One letter stated that unidentified parties might have decided to sink the *Don* and that Captain Johnson was unaware of the plot.

Another letter gave a weird theory, and concluded as follows: "It's just too fantastic to believe, but I know."

Another writer said with assurance that a German U-boat sank the *Don*. The letter was based on the fact that the writer had picked up a bag of "brim" with a German inscription on it, at or near Bailey Island.

I would not dare print some of the letters I have received, because of the almost unbelievable implications. The reader of this chapter must be satisfied with the following quotes from four different letters:

A U-boat sent the *Don* to the bottom under the cover of fog. It had waited between Monhegan Island and the mainland for an appropriate time and victim.

A mine which had been placed at the entrance to Halifax Harbor to keep out the German submarines broke from its moorings, drifted down the coast, and blew up when it bumped against the hull of the *Don*.

There is something about the disappearance of the thirty-four people and the *Don* which is so mysterious, and so far-fetched from reality, that in my opinion the disaster will never be solved. If it is solved and the truth in all its strangeness comes out, no one will believe it anyway.

The loss of the *Don* will always be an enigma. I have heard so many rumors from so many sources, that I now believe that the entire affair, horrible as it is to say so, was planned from beginning to end. There are greater forces than we can understand at the back of the disaster, and the average person will never know the truth which has been known for some time by certain residents of Casco Bay.

On August 2, 1963, the bow of the *Don* was brought up by fishermen Bernard Johnson and John Lazarou near Round Rock, Casco Bay, where they had been dragging on a well-known course. Suddenly, as Johnson expressed it, the drag went off into deep water "involving a point of no return." The drag was hauled up and wreckage which Johnson readily recognized was found. Much debris was in the bow, such as foot gear and binoculars.

When the fog cleared the draggermen discovered that their course had not been the one they had planned to take, and this is the only reason the drag fastened on the remains of the *Don*.

Fisherman Johnson recalled that one of his associates, on the night the *Don* disappeared, had heard what apparently was the *Don* attempting to get off the Round Rock Ledge, where she probably had grounded in the fog. The other fisherman remembered that the motor raced violently, as though the captain of the *Don* was doing everything he could to slide off the rocky area.

PART THREE

Pirates and Buried Treasure

1

Dixie Bull

We will probably never know who Casco Bay's first pirate was, but the name of Dixie Bull should undoubtedly be considered and could easily be given highest place in any American listing of Who's Who in New England piracy. Fortunately for the reader interested in pirate history, men like John Winthrop, William Bradford, and Captain Roger Clap were fond of writing about the daily occurrences of their times, for otherwise the man I would like to call the first pirate in Casco Bay would be practically unknown.

What we have discovered about Dixie Bull is at best sketchy, but it has been established that he was living in London in 1631, one year after the settlement of Boston by the Puritans. In the fall of that year he arrived at Boston and stayed for several months. It seems probable that this young man was sent over to America by Sir Ferdinando Gorges. At least we know that he is mentioned with Gorges in a land grant at York, Maine. Bull came from an extremely respectable family in England, and is called by historians George F. Dow and John H. Edmonds a man of "adventurous disposition." This should not necessarily condemn him, but his disposition rapidly changed from adventurous to piratical, and all this came about because of the French.

Soon after reaching New England, Dixie Bull became a beaver trader and seemed to enjoy the life. His forays took him up and down the beautiful coast of Maine, from York to what is now Yarmouth. He was a friend of the white settlers who had established themselves there, and he also seemed to get along well with the Indians. The Pilgrim trading post at Penobscot Bay was one of his favorite visiting places, and Richmond Island knew him well.

This situation changed, however, with the arrival of some Frenchmen. The Pilgrim traders often journeyed inland from trading posts with their supplies of coats, blankets, biscuits, and the like, which they would exchange for beaver pelts and otter skins, leaving the settlement in the charge of a small group of men. One day, when they had left for the interior of Maine, a French shallop was seen approaching the shore. A man on the French vessel called to the Pilgrims in English, imitating the accent of a Scotchman. He explained that the shallop had just arrived from a long journey, and its passengers knew not where they were. Claiming that the vessel was leaking badly, he asked permission to bring her up on the beach at low tide for repairs.

The Pilgrims agreed, and the Frenchmen, after pulling their shallop up, went over to the trading post, where they found conditions ideal for their plans. Only four men were left at the post. Seeing racks of guns and muskets on the walls, the Frenchmen examined them carefully, complimenting the Pilgrims on their fine workmanship. Suddenly, however, the Frenchmen held up the four Pilgrims, using the trading post's own guns. After rifling the post of some three or four hundred pounds' worth of merchandise, they sailed away, telling the four unfortunate Pilgrims to inform their masters that gentlemen from the Island of Rhe had called.

Whether or not Dixie Bull knew of this depredation at the time is not known. Sometime later, however, while he was sailing off the Maine coast, he sighted a French pinnace, which engaged him and captured his shallop, took all his supplies, and left him destitute. This was in June, 1632.

Dixie Bull tried manfully to get his revenge on the French pirates. Organizing a small band of fifteen men, he sailed along the coastline, hoping to catch some French vessel and thus retrieve his losses. As the summer months waned and his own supplies dwindled, Bull realized that something would have to be done soon.

His next move was one that should establish him as the first New England pirate in recorded history. Descending on the pinnaces and shallops of some defenseless English traders located nearby, Dixie Bull confiscated their supplies and forced several men from the traders' vessels to join his pirate band.

Thus reinforced, Captain Dixie Bull sailed brazenly across into Pemaquid Harbor, where he looted the settlement at his leisure, as there was no opposition of any importance. Bull and his cohorts loaded merchandise aboard their shallop to the value of more than five hundred pounds, leaving the inhabitants stunned. The exception was a small group of armed men. These defenders sent a parting volley out toward the pirate ship just as the ruffians weighed anchor to sail off with their booty. One of the bullets scored a lucky hit, killing Captain Bull's second in command.

The death of the pirate caused a terrific reaction from his fellow sailors, as this was actually the first bloodshed any of them had encountered. None had ever served before on a piratical voyage, and it was a long time before the effects of the incident wore off. Captain Roger Clap, who was commander at Castle Island in Boston Harbor for many years, interviewed several of the men some time later. Clap said that the pirates were so upset weeks afterward that they were afraid of the "very rattling of the ropes."*

News of Dixie Bull's piracy reached Boston via a dispatch from Walter Neal of Piscataqua, who wrote a letter to Governor John Winthrop describing the incidents that led to Bull's becoming a sea highwayman. Neal asked Winthrop to send an armed vessel with twenty men up the coast to Piscataqua, now Portsmouth, to search for Bull. The officials underwent a great deal of trouble getting the expedition organized, and then the weather interfered. First snow, then extreme cold, and finally contrary winds prevented the sailing. An interesting sidelight on the expedition is the fact that Samuel Maverick, mentioned years before in the York Deeds along with Dixie Bull, actually was the man chosen to outfit the expedition to capture him.

At last, late in November, the expedition left Boston. A well-armed pinnace started up the coast with twenty strong marines aboard. Sailing through Casco Bay, they eventually reached Pemaquid, where the pinnace was joined by four other heavily armed vessels, one of which was from "Pascataquack." Weather conditions then interfered again, and for the next three weeks the ships lay storm-bound.

Historians should note that this force was the first armed fleet ever outfitted in New England, as well as perhaps the first to perform a naval demonstration in the Colonies.

Nevertheless, nothing ever came of the efforts of these brave men of Massachusetts and Maine. Week after week went by while they thoroughly searched Casco Bay, but they were unable to find Dixie Bull. Finally the fleet left the shores of Maine and returned to Piscataqua, New Hampshire, where the sailors were disbanded. Lieutenant Mason, leader of the expedition, was given ten pounds for his services, while the other expenses came to twenty-four pounds seven shillings.

In February, 1633, three deserters from Dixie Bull's pirate

*Roger Clap, *Memoirs*, p. 35.

fleet reached their homes. They believed that Dixie Bull had left American waters forever, crossing the Atlantic to fight for the French. Writing in his journal two years later, Governor John Winthrop was of the same opinion. Captain Roger Clap of Dorchester, who interviewed the men, believed that Dixie Bull eventually reached England. In Clap's words: "Bull got to England; but God destroyed this wretched man. Thus the Lord saved us at this time, from their wicked Device against us."

Bull probably was executed or met a violent death in England. Regardless of how he died, so far as we know America never again saw the man who was destined to wear the mantle of New England's first pirate.

Of course, it would be hard to convince the average state of Mainer that Dixie Bull did not die in the manner in which the ancient ode called "The Slaying of Dixey Bull" indicates. The ballad was sung for more than a century from an old broadside which probably was printed in Falmouth around 1825.

Excerpts from the poem, which might have been written by a Longfellow of an earlier generation, follow:

> THE SLAYING OF DIXEY BULL
> Dixey Bull was a pirate bold,
> He swept our coast in search of gold,
> One hundred years have passed away
> Since he cast anchor in Bristol Bay.
> Under the lea of Beaver's shore
> He laid his craft three days or more;
> He flaunted his flag and shot his lead,
> Which kept the people out of bed.
> Until the folks of old Jamestown
> Had passed the word to all around
> That Dixey Bull, the pirate bold,
> Would not leave without their gold.

Into the fort the people came
To fight this man of bloody fame;
But well they knew the fort would fall
When stormed by powder and by ball.
Their gold was gathered in a pile
To send to him at Beaver's Isle,
So the pirate would go his way
And leave the waters of Bristol Bay.
But Daniel Curtis, a fisherman,
Feared not the flag from which they ran,
But took his skiff; bent to his oar,
And rowed alone to Beaver's shore.
'I, Dan Curtis, my boat will pull
Down to the craft of Dixey Bull
And man to man, we'll meet tonight,
To settle for all in good fair fight.'
The women wept, the children cried,
As he went off to the pirate's side,
He gave a roar and waved his hand,
And said, 'I want to see the man,
The captain of this bloody crew,
Then I'll tell him what I will do.'
Bold was the pirate, Dixey Bull,
Said he, 'Of fight I am chuck full.
I'm the man your shores doth haunt;
Blood or your gold is what I want.
I will bleed for my country's sake
And for the gold put up a stake.
Then single handed you and I
Shall fight until the other die.'
Then Daniel Curtis rose and said,
'All right till you or I am dead.'
Down to the belt the fighters strip,
O'er the sod commenced to skip,

Touched their swords and gave a twist,
To test the strength of each other's wrist.
A cut now falls on Dixey's neck
And groans rise from the pirate's deck—
The people cheer their Daniel brave,
As he their gold is going to save.
Dixey Bull a new trick tried,
Laying deep his sword in Curtis' side,
But Curtis, brave as a man can be,
Laughed at their cheers of three times three.
Dixey raised his sword on high
Which flashed like lightning in the sky,
He thought his man was nearly dead,
So gave a sweep to cut his head.
As Dixey's sword was falling down
Curtis sprang up from the ground
In front of him by many feet
Went Dixey's cruel deadly sweep.
Like a flash at him Dan went
And through his breast his sword he sent,
The blood gushed out warm, bright and red,
The pirate staggered and fell dead
Then like a stream rushed Dixey's gore
O'er Beaver's bleak and rocky shore;
When they saw that the fight was done
The people cheered because they'd won.
Pirates, your flag and anchor pull,
For Curtis killed your Dixey Bull.
That's how Curtis won the day
And killed his man in Bristol Bay.
He saved the gold and saved the town,
And won a name of great renown,
The skull and cross bones which they flew
Was then dipped by the pirate's crew.

Their anchor then was weighed o'er rail,
And gentle wind then filled their sail,
While cannons rang and cheers were given
They left for good old Bristol's haven.

2

The *Albion Cooper* Pirates

For well over twelve years I have been receiving mail from interested people who have studied the Casco Bay map which artist Draper Hill and I designed and produced. The letters mostly concern a sketch showing the sailing vessel *Albion Cooper*. In the drawing three men have just been thrown overboard.

Since the map was made I have been given substantial help with the story of the *Albion Cooper* by Mrs. Laura Lancaster of Auburn, Maine, whose background in Maine history is outstanding. A visit to the Auburn-Lewistown area at the time of a lecture a few years ago also increased my knowledge of the tragedy.

The *Albion Cooper* sailed for Cuba from Portland on July 27, 1857, carrying a load of lumber consigned to the firm of Bedel and Nephew of Cardenas, which is located about seventy-five miles east of Havana. Neither the ship nor any of her officers were destined to return to Casco Bay.

The ship's company consisted of Captain Daniel R. Humphrey; First Mate Collingwood P. Smith; Second Mate Quinton

D. Smith; Cook Abraham Cox, sixty-eight years old, a black native of Kennebunk; Peter Williams, alias William Harvey, twenty-seven years old; David Burns; and sixteen-year-old Thomas Lahey.

Almost before Portland Head Light was astern, rumblings of unhappiness began, a quarrel between the first mate and the cook. By the end of the week First Mate Smith was finding fault all around the galley, usually considered the cook's exclusive domain. Objecting to the manner in which the cook stored the food, the mate tipped over a sack of peas to prove his point. Smith then blamed the cook for putting the bag in the way. When Cox began to explain the reason for putting the peas where he did, he was greeted with a terrific blow over the left eye.

Cox later reported his mistreatment to Captain Humphrey, hoping to get either sympathy or satisfaction. He received neither, for the captain replied that he would have no quarreling aboard at any time, and told the cook in no uncertain terms that officers should always be obeyed.

Seeking consolation, Cox solicited the friendship of Seaman Williams, and the two men then and there agreed to band together in a plot which would develop into mutiny and piracy unless there was a decided change toward leniency in the officers' treatment of the crew.

Shortly afterward the captain spoke to the mate, but whether the captain told the mate to bear down harder or to ease off will never be known. The result, unfortunately, was that the mate tormented the cook more than ever until his abuse became unbearable.

Matters reached a head on August 20, 1857, when the mate definitely went out of his way to find fault with the meal, suggesting that Cox's preparation of the food had reduced it to slop.

Cox answered vehemently, stoutly defending himself, whereupon Smith knocked the unfortunate Cox down with a violent blow.

That very evening Smith, who had noticed Williams and the cook fraternizing at various times, stepped over to Williams and accused the seaman of slighting his obligations as a sailor.

"You'd better get up on deck and finish your work," ordered First Mate Smith, but the seaman had other ideas.

"I finish my supper first," came the answer, and for the second time that day, the huge fist of the mate smashed into the face of a member of the *Albion Cooper*'s crew. The battered Williams retreated into the forecastle.

The mate, sensing that he might have trouble on his hands, reported at once to Captain Humphrey, telling him what had taken place.

The two officers went forward. The mate called to Williams to come out of the forecastle, but Williams refused.

"You'd better leave me alone," Williams cried, "or we'll all be sorry. Go away and let me be." Williams was simply crazy with anger at having been abused and struck by his superior officer.

After a brief conference with the captain, the mate and the second officer entered the forecastle. They seized the sailor and dragged him out on deck. In the presence of the captain, the mate struck the seaman, knocked him down, jumped on him, and then kicked him. The injured Williams threatened the mate in no uncertain language.

Drawing his sheath knife, Mate Smith stabbed at Williams, managing to give the sailor a glancing blow in the breast, after which the captain and the two mates left the unhappy man on the deck.

The officers then conferred, deciding to put Williams in irons in spite of his stab wound, which proved to be superficial. Reaching the forecastle, the master again ordered Williams to come out.

"I'll come out if you promise, Captain, not to hit me or hurt me again," was the reply of Williams.

"I promise not to strike you," Captain Humphrey answered, whereupon the sailor came out on deck, was put in irons, taken below deck, and locked in the brig.

When morning came Williams was released. Told to work the pumps, the sailor refused. At noon he was given a piece of bread and a small amount of water.

Williams continued his refusal to work, whereupon First Mate Smith decided to take matters into his own hands. Getting a sledge and a spike, he drove the spike into the beam of his stateroom. He then had Williams brought in and handcuffed him. Smith now placed a sea chest under the spike and forced Williams to climb up on the chest. He raised the sailor's handcuffed arms high in the air until the handcuffs fitted over the spike and then withdrew the chest, leaving Williams dangling in the air.

Hour after hour passed, until at noon the following day Williams was cut down by the second mate and allowed to stumble forward to his bunk.

Later, when visited by First Mate Smith, Williams spoke to the superior officer.

"Why don't you just kill me and be done with it?" he questioned. "Why continue punishing me?"

"That answer is easy, for we have further hardships for you," came the reply. A short time later Williams was returned to the mate's quarters and again placed in handcuffs and left hanging from the spike in the beam. "This is a small penalty compared to what is coming," were the mate's words as he left the unfortunate seaman swinging in the air.

At four o'clock the next morning Williams was taken down and allowed to return to his quarters in the forecastle. He was permitted to lie in his bunk, but with his handcuffs still on.

At the first opportunity Cox visited Williams, who talked

with the cook about revenge. The two men decided to kill the officers and become pirates. However, their plan was weak in one vital aspect. Neither man could read or write, and neither had the ability to navigate the *Albion Cooper*. They must have someone else on whom they could depend.

Thomas Lahey, sixteen years of age, had a fair education, could read and write, and seemed an affable lad. Could they discuss his ability with him? The opportunity for a conference came when the *Albion Cooper* was becalmed on the Bahama Banks.

It was August 28, 1857. The schemers asked Lahey about his capability in navigation, and the youth admitted that in an emergency he could probably chart a course and navigate the *Albion Cooper*. The questions of the two men, however, aroused Lahey's suspicions.

Shortly after midnight that very evening, when Lahey was forward on watch, Cox and Williams began their terrible act of piracy. With razors, axes, and hatchets, they started out in search of their victims, which included all three officers on board and Seaman David Burns.

Williams entered the captain's cabin. The sailor saw the master asleep in his bunk, and then and there killed Captain Humphrey with one blow of his hatchet. Williams heard the first mate, who had been awakened by the commotion, yelling from his bunk. Blood-stained weapon in hand, the seaman hid at the top of the companion hatchway to await Smith's appearance.

When First Mate Smith reached the companion, Williams brought the hatchet down on Smith's head, knocking the officer to the deck but not killing him.

Abraham Cox had been assigned the task of killing Second Mate Quinton Smith at the same time that Williams was disposing of the first mate. Reaching the quarters of the second mate, Cox stumbled over a cask, making just enough noise to awaken Smith.

"What are you doing here?" came the question.

"I was told to trim the night lamp," Cox replied.

"You are not doing it," answered Mate Smith. "I don't believe you." Cox then swung his axe, killing the officer with two blows.

By this time Lahey had heard the noise and he called for Seaman David Burns to come out on deck. But Williams and Cox ran toward Lahey, telling him to stop his shouts or they would have to kill him as well.

Cox now picked up the large axe, and took a position by the galley door. Williams forced a lantern into Lahey's hands, grabbed a razor, and then the two pirates approached the sleeping Burns. Both men struck, leaving Burns in a terrible condition, but David Burns did not die until the forenoon of the following day.

The two murderers soon began to wonder if First Mate Smith had actually been killed. They went to the officer, who was lying on his side. Cox spoke to Smith, who was able to answer him, and then and there the pirates ended Smith's life.

It was now necessary to deal with the dead. Cox and Williams, aided by the shocked Lahey, attached heavy chains to the four bodies, sewed them inside canvas tarpaulins, and placed the murdered victims at the stern taffrail.

The terrible act of consigning the slain men to the sea was carried out, the only witnesses being the two pirates and sixteen-year-old Lahey.

The real hero of the entire affair was the boy Thomas Lahey. Faced with an overwhelming responsibility for a youth of such relatively tender years, Lahey decided that there was only one thing to do. Having noticed that the cloak of the second mate was his size, the lad decided to keep it and hide in its lining the log of the *Albion Cooper*, which was recorded in a small notebook.

Lahey's next act was to write into the logbook his name, the place where he was born, the name of the *Albion Cooper*, the day when the murders had been committed, and the names of the sailors who had carried out the four piratical acts of mur- der. Lahey then placed the log inside the lining of the cloak and sewed the garment up again.

For three days and three nights Lahey navigated the *Albion Cooper*, but at the end of the third night the two pirates decided that they should set fire to the craft, abandon her in a small boat, and wait to be picked up.

Lahey now realized that the two pirates were planning to murder him at the first chance, for he could reveal their guilt if allowed to stay alive. Nevertheless, when they told him to help load the small boat, he did so, and by the time he finished getting the supplies aboard, the others had set fire to the *Albion Cooper*. All three climbed into the small boat as the *Cooper* began to burn. Checking again the supplies aboard the boat, they pushed away from the blazing brig.

About an hour later, the three men sighted a large vessel and attempted to reach it, but in spite of lightening their craft of supplies and rowing at top speed, they were outdistanced, and they watched as the ship disappeared over the horizon.

Two more craft came into view that afternoon, followed by two others the next morning, but all passed by without noticing the small boat.

Finally a brig, the *Black Squall* of Philadelphia, bound to Havana, overtook them, and they were rescued. As soon as he could, Lahey asked for and received a private conference with the master of the *Black Squall*. Pulling the mate's cloak from his duffle bag, the young man cut open the lining and showed the captain the logbook.

The captain treated the pirates with consideration until reaching Cuba, where he turned the two men over to the United States Consul. Arrangements were made for all three survivors to be sent on the bark *R. H. Wright* to Portland, Maine.

A strange mystery, never solved, developed. Three days before the *Wright* reached Portland, Lahey was found dead and was given a sea burial. It has always been suspected that in some way the two pirates caused his death, but no proof of this has ever been discovered.

In January, 1858, at Auburn, Maine, the two surviving members of the crew of the *Albion Cooper* were taken from the jail where they had been incarcerated, to the district court of the United States. Judge Asher Ware presided, with District Attorney George F. Shepley the prosecutor, and George F. Evans appearing for the defendants.

On January 20, 1858, a verdict of guilty was returned against the two pirates. Peter Williams (also known as William Harvey) and Abraham Cox were sentenced to be hanged on August 27, 1858. On that day, before a large crowd gathered across from the jail yard in Auburn, the two men were swung out into eternity.

On the day of the execution an almost-forgotten custom was revived, the selling of a broadside on the streets of Auburn to the waiting crowd.

I quote from the broadside, which was written by O. K. Yates. The first verses concern Williams.

> Indulgent friends pray list awhile
> While I a few things relate
> Concerning we poor criminals
> And our unhappy fate.
>
> One missionary a little girl
> That came and read to me;
> God bless her for her precious words
> Brought me my sins to see.
>
> But there's one friend who stands by me
> 'Bove father, mother, all;

'Tis Christ, to friend to such as me,
To sinners this loudly calls.

Ye captains all, one word to you,
While you sail on the seas,
See that your men are not abused
And wronged so shamefully.

Sailors, do not as I have done
It's better to suffer more,
If consuls will not hear your plea,
Then leave while you're on shore.

Altho the mate, he knocked me down
And hung me by my wrists,
Better suffer this and even more
Than officers to resist.

My days I number by the year
Now months and weeks pass by,
And now appears that fatal day,
That I'm led out to die.

Farewell, vain world, I bid adieu!
Farewell those friends so kind;
Be cautious how you're led astray,
Into folly, vice and crime.

The poetry concerning Cox follows:

On St. Martin's Island I was born,
Twelve years was I a slave;
My mistress she was kind to me
And to me my freedom gave.

Soon after that I went to sea
On the southern coast did sail,

Four years I went before the mast,
Then withstood the roughest gale.

Seaman when you are treated harsh
You'd better bear the pain;
If you resist you'll suffer more,
And nothing will you gain.

The wife I've loved with all my heart
To me has cruel proved;
Our little ones she has turned off,
She'll not my troubles soothe.

Today she lives with another man
By him has children two;
She is the cause of what I am,
This I declare is true

I should have been today in trade,
And quit the roving sea,
I'd ample means to invest in trade,—
To that she'd not agree.

I've suffered much the ills of life,
'Till my years are sixty-eight;
With crippling limbs and tottering frame,
I'm led to the gallows gate.

The time has come, when I must tread,
That solemn gallows floor;
This crippled form and my grey head,
Will suffer but little more.

Farewell my wife, whom I forgive;
Farewell my children dear,
Farewell this world where I have lived
Before Christ I soon appear.

3

Smugglers and Privateers
of Jewel Island

There were many more pirates, smugglers, and privateers on the Maine coast than the average person realizes. Hundreds of tiny coves, inlets, and harbors of the Pine Tree State offered many tempting opportunities for this sort of maritime activity.

Piracy is the capture of men or ships at sea in peacetime; privateering is the same activity in wartime. Smuggling is the illegal transportation of goods and commodities into or out of an area or country in any time, war or peace, and is usually carried out to avoid the payment of customs duties.

If we concentrate our history on just one individual island in Casco Bay, Jewel Island, across from Cliff Island, probably has had as much smuggling, rum-running, and privateering as any other area along the coast, maybe even more, and there are substantial indications that one or two cases of unproved piracy occurred there.

At the turn of the century and again during the present generation, items that suggest illegal activity have been found on the island. In 1903 a group of workmen were making extensive repairs in the basement of the old farmhouse on the island where Captain Jonathan Chase lived. As they remodeled the area under the colonial kitchen of the house, one of the workers suddenly gave a yell, for he found himself dropping with his pick down into a long dark passageway that had collapsed under his efforts.

Work stopped at once, and the other laborers gathered around John Sawtelle, the workman whose pick had found the passageway. Getting a torch, he lighted it and the others followed him at a respectful distance. They reached the end of the tunnel, which led out to the cove in back of the house. The results of their hike were many. They discovered that when the tide was out, the entire passageway was clear, but when high tide arrived, the sea filled the tunnel about half the length.

The laborers learned that when high tide arrived, strange noises began to come from that section of the passageway still above water. Uncle Sam Pettengill later testified that he had heard those noises on several occasions, especially when he was working for Captain Chase. Although others attempted to explain the noises by references to geology and possible wind-vent disturbances such as are heard at other locations along the Maine coast, Uncle Sam always refused to accept their theories.

"Down in this cellar," Sam explained, "I often stored potatoes for the winter, and I have seen with my own eyes curious places which must have been built by the hand of man for the purpose of smuggling or other even more nefarious practice. Along by the wall of the cellar there were great underground holes or pockets, some as large as the cellar of an ordinary house and others not larger than a barrel. From these pockets to the beach of the cove was only a short carry by means of the underground passage. At dead low water it was possible to smuggle in tons and tons of goods without anyone being the wiser.

"I think that much liquor from foreign lands and lands not so foreign must have been stored in the cellar pockets of that old farmhouse. At that time, probably in the 1740's, '50's, and '60's, there was more money in liquor smuggling than anything else.

"When I was only a baby, as my mother told me, a man by the name of St. Claire hired the island. No one here knew where he came from. All that we could find out was that he carried on a business of leaching out copper from the mineral which abounds on the island. St. Claire lived to be a very old man, but how long he stayed on the island I do not know.

"My father, Nathaniel Pettengill, was born on Jewel's Island in a house that used to stand just back of the old farmhouse. I have heard Father tell about the different men who came to dig for the treasure which was believed to be buried there. Some of them had bottles of lambs' blood. They sprinkled it all around the place where they wanted to dig in a complete circle. This was to keep out the Devil or Old Kiff or some of his followers from Cliff Island while they hunted for the treasure.

"Legends and traditions I have often listened to, but my own experiences regarding a wanderer from the sea who arrived in a small sloop or schooner have always haunted me. When he landed to dig for treasure, his activities fascinated my youthful imagination, and he quickly won my friendship. His name was Mark Conliff.

"Well, I fixed up a room for Conliff in the eastern end of the old farmhouse, and I soon learned that his mind was continually occupied with the money that he would find. Every night before he went to bed he had a habit of kneeling down and praying that he would find the treasure the next day.

"One night he went to bed later than usual after having put in a very long and unsuccessful day in trying to locate the spot of the buried gold. It was about a week, by the way, before old Captain Chase appeared on the scene and I saw Conliff alive for the last time. Well, as Conliff told me later, he went to sleep quick enough but along in the middle of the night he was awakened by the opening of his bedroom door. Someone, he felt sure, was creeping into his room as steadily as a cat, and he sat bolt upright in bed and stared straight at the door to see who it could be.

"First a man's head came into view, then his body, and then his legs as far down as the knees.

"He was very stout with light hair and beard and 'as broad as old Uncle Chase's cookstove,' as Conliff expressed it. He glided rather than walked up to Conliff's bedside. Then Conliff moved over and sat on the edge of the bed nearest the door. This of course brought Conliff so close to him that he could have stretched out his hand and touched him. But he didn't do anything of the kind. He felt that this was the man who knew all about the treasure—in fact, he was sure of it, but to find the words to question him, he couldn't. Three times he moistened his parched lips to put a question, and each time the words failed him. But each time the man smiled and nodded his head encouragingly. Finally, just as the words seemed to come to him from afar, the man or ghost or whatever-it-was turned and glided out of the door with a laugh.

"Now Conliff was a silent man, not given to storytelling in any sense. He told me that this thing that happened to him was God's truth. All I know is that every night after he told me that story he prayed that the man would again visit him in his room, but he never did.

"As regards the treasure, so far as I could ever find out, Pond Cove on the island is the most likely place for it. You take a mineral rod and go over there and you will find that there is a wonderful attraction. It is believed that Old Kiff or some of his pirates were trying to beach their ship in a storm when there came a big sea which wrecked the ship and overturned the treasure into a deep hole in the cove. One day when I happened to be on the island, I took a mineral rod down there myself and there was such an attraction that I could not hold it!

"There's another place on Jewel's Island where some say the pirates buried their treasure, this time by careful planning. I could not take you to the exact spot today, but if I had the map which was given to Conliff by an old man, I think I could do so. This particular band of pirates dug a place on high land away from the wear of the tide and lined it with French brick, which made a regular vault out of it. Then they piled in their treasure in heavy iron sea chests. After the last chest was in position, they summoned the entire crew of the ship and placed an enormous flat rock on top of the vault. Soon after this it was said that the entire crew and all of the pirates except two of the leaders were lost at sea by the sudden scuttling of the ship.*

"Two large letters were cut in the rock. I heard my father say that he had seen them and wondered over them often when he had been farming on the island. Since my father lived on the island I heard of those mysterious letters on several occasions, so I have reason to believe that they must serve as a sort of guide to the location of the treasure.

"About the year 1900 one of our Maine sea captains of South Freeport made a trip to Philadelphia in a certain coaster of which he was master.

"Among the places that he visited while in Philadelphia was an eating house frequented by sea captains. Here he met a very old, retired sea captain, who in the course of the conversation asked him if he ever cruised much of any along the Maine coast.

" 'Yes,' answered the South Freeport captain, 'I come from Maine.'

" 'Do you happen to know of an island by the name of Jewel's?' the other inquired.

" 'Oh, yes, I live only a few miles from that island.'

*A similar tale involves the *Whidah* at Cape Cod, with 143 drowned, 2 saved, on April 26, 1717.

"Well, to make a long story short, the old sea captain told the story of the vault of French brick and the big rock and the letters on it just as I have told it to you. Finally the old man confessed that he was one of the pirates who escaped from the scuttled ship, and he named over the letters cut on the rocks and explained what they meant. 'I will never need the treasure,' said he, 'for I am getting too old and will die before the year is out. I will give it to you and you can do with it what you will!'

"The Freeport captain died less than a year later," Uncle Sam sorrowfully stated. "He was never seen on the island, but he was intending to visit it in order to take possession of his own the very summer he passed away.

"There are places on Jewel's Island which cannot be fully explained by any living man," resumed Uncle Samuel. "I believe that someone someday will strike it rich, for I have no reason to doubt the strange tales of the island and its treasure trove."

Although the treasure is still in the vault with the rock above it, Sam and his associates never really attempted systematic research to find the treasure. I believe they were too superstitious, and a resident concurs with me in that belief.

4

Pirate Treasure and
John Sylvester

Now that dreams have been accepted as a means of understanding yourself better, it is possible that dreams of finding pirate treasure may offer a greater challenge. Patricia Garfield tells us in *Creative Dreaming* that by planning your dreams you may get increased self-awareness and the solution to personal and business problems. From a practical viewpoint, definite dream organization for finding pirate treasure might have some very interesting results.

Whether or not it would have helped John Sylvester in Casco Bay will never be known, but his wife, Martha, always believed until the time of his death that his efforts to find the treasure he dreamed of time and again would be successful. I have heard parts of the story from five different sources, and evidently there was quite a little excitement when the tale became generally known about fifty years ago.*

*When I talked with Herbert Jones in 1951 he gave me much information he did not include in his book *Isles of Casco Bay*. Incidentally, I have utterly failed to identify John Sylvester in genealogical sources. Margaret Burr Todd mentions Charles Sylvester, who had a poultry farm on Pond Island.

One September night in his home on Bailey Island John Sylvester sat upright in bed and shook his wife's shoulder, whispering excitedly to her that he had had a dream. His wife simply grunted and rolled over, turning her back. But John was determined to talk to her.

"Martha," he began, "that dream is important. I'm going to Portland in the morning."

Martha realized that John was showing a little more energy than usual, and rolled back toward him.

"What on earth for?"

"I told you I had a dream. You remember when brother Len and I were boys, that pirate-looking fellow who got Father to row him across to Pond Island? Well, in the dream I just had I saw him and Injun Bessie lifting a big treasure chest out of the ground, and it was full of gold. I'm going across to Portland and see Injun Bessie. I bet she'll tell me where on Pond Island that treasure is buried!"

"Keep away from Injun Bessie, John, or I might start trouble. I remember your story of the swarthy ruffian wearing a red bandanna and gold earrings. I've heard it a thousand times, and that's a thousand times too many. Keep away from Injun Bessie. As you tell the story the pirate never found the treasure, so why do you think that Injun Bessie can do any better? No Indian fortune-teller can really help you."

"Well," answered John, "I'm going up to see her anyway."

"How about doing something practical like getting a berth on Frank Sterling's smack?"

"I could do that."

"You could, but you won't. I heard there was a thirty-two-dollar share last trip, only three days out!"

"I know all that. Maybe I will go fishing, but I am going to see Injun Bessie first." And that was the way the discussion ended.

Shortly after that both fell asleep. When a night wind came

up, the surf across Mink Rocks echoed in through their open
window and soon awakened John. He had drifted off again into
his dream of finding the treasure on Pond Island. This time in
his dream, after finding the treasure he moved into a splendid
brownstone residence on State Street in the very heart of Portland, a mansion with an attractive lawn, a superb fountain with
pond lilies and goldfish as well, and a statue of a great dog
standing out in front of the house.

When he left his mansion in the morning, he would be wearing "a snowy white stock and black coat similar to that worn
by Judge Baxter and on top of his head would be a stovepipe
hat, even shinier than Mr. Deering's!" He would be everything
then that he was not now, a respected man of importance when
he gave his opinion of "the cause of storms or the best way to
break up a setting hen." He would become president of the First
National Bank, and his former fellow islanders would arrive at
the bank for a loan, "twisting their sea caps in their hands,"
pledging their homes against their chances of fishing for gain.

Indeed, John would make storekeeper Moody sweat for
refusing him credit, and he would foreclose the mortgage on
Ed Green's house for laughing at him when he tried to stop an
old Plymouth hen from hatching out fourteen good eggs.

Suddenly he came out of his reverie. He realized dawn was
near, and he had planned to go to Portland with Ed Green in
the dory in less than an hour and a half.

It was now light enough to make out the dressing stand
across the bedroom, and then he heard a cock crow. Shortly
afterward John slipped out of bed, dressed, and went downstairs to renew the kitchen fire and start the coffee.

Thirty minutes later, after eating eggs and drinking three
cups of coffee, he took a paper bag and put in a good supply
of bread and doughnuts. Then he went to the hen yard and
counted out thirty-six eggs, which he placed in a sturdy recepta-
cle, and left the house without disturbing Martha.

Soon he was outside neighbor Ed Green's home, where he knocked on the kitchen door. Invited in, he asked his red-headed friend if he might be Portland-bound. The reply came in the affirmative, and John asked if he could go along. Another affirmative answer resulted.

A short time later both men were loading lobsters into the dory. Soon there were four brimming barrels of the tempting crustaceans, and the two men cast off for Portland in a spanking breeze. After they left shore they noticed, across on Jewel Island, Sam Pettengill* painting his house. Later, sailing off Long Island, they ran by the Stepping Stones, where John was amazed at the myriads of lobster buoys he saw there. It seemed that everyone was fishing that fall.

Ed sat at the tiller, speculating on the price of lobsters as the dory was steered over the shorter course through the passageway between Pumpkin Nob and Peak's Island.

Reaching Trefethen's Wharf in Portland, they unloaded the lobsters, and John had a question to ask Ed.

"When are you starting back?"

"About eleven o'clock, if it's all right with you."

There seemed to be a little sarcasm in Ed's voice.

John nodded and walked away, carrying his eggs over to Boyce's General Store, where he received thirty-six cents for the three dozen eggs. This sum was the only money he then had with him.

Well aware that Injun Bessie, the fortune-teller, lived in a relatively small building near Mr. Longfellow's house, John headed at once for her home. When he sighted the fortune-teller's quarters, however, he began to have misgivings. He recalled Deacon Orr's powerful, thundering sermon against witchcraft and clairvoyants to which he had listened years before, and he thought of how he had sneaked away that morn-

*The Pettengill family, off and on, resided on both Cliff and Jewel Islands.

ing, leaving Martha sleeping upstairs. He knew that everyone claimed that the fortune-teller had "entered into an unholy, carnal alliance with the Evil One himself," and that Charity Skillings had been bewitched by a fortune-teller to go out of her senses and jump overboard one day.

John's courage had now nearly left him, but slowly the lure of gold brought it back. He raised his hand and rapped on the door. It opened, and there was Injun Bessie. She had never been pretty, and now in advanced age, her face brown and wrinkled, she resembled a "dried cherry." Her great hooked nose did nothing to improve her looks, and the dark eyes under heavy black brows glowered at him.

"What you want?" came the hollow, sepulchral voice.

John explained that he wished her to relate his fortune.

The fortune-teller pointed to a small room, into which John stepped. There he found a floor "strewn with hides, deer, moose, and bear; and on the walls hung more hides, wampum belts, long strings of conch shells, stone hatchets, and knives with clamshell blades, head-dresses of feather, and charms of heron wings, and curiously worked spirit bags."*

In the middle of the tiny room was a low table covered with a black cloth on which stood a great rock crystal, jagged and rough, which glistened in the morning light. The ancient squaw motioned for John to sit down.

"I want wampum," she demanded. John handed her a quarter.

"More wampum," came her next demand. John shook his head, but when she again asked for money he gave her a dime and a new penny. He then spread out his hands, indicating that he had given her his total wealth.

For a moment she debated what to do. Then she deposited the thirty-six cents in her bosom and looked across at the

*Williams Haynes, *Casco Bay Yarns*, p. 29.

islander. Finally closing her eyes, Bessie bowed her head as if in prayer.

John wondered whether at that moment she was actually communicating with her satanic lover, as Deacon Orr had hinted in his sermon years before, but suddenly Injun Bessie began to sway and started to chant in a shrill falsetto which sent shivers down John's spine.

"I see canoe with wings, you and another come to Portland, other with red hair. Me see you and other brave go to island, island where brave and his nine brothers and two sisters all play. You have shovels, with other brave go same island, take shovels and dig big, big chest, full gold, heaps gold, heaps wampum. He never find, you never find, but together you find. Go, that is all," and she pointed at the door.

A moment later John stood blinking in the sunlight. By "big chest" did Injun Bessie mean the same chest he had seen in his dream? The red-haired brave was, of course, red-headed Ed Green, and the winged canoe was Ed's sailing dory. Ed and his brothers and sisters were all born on Pond Island, and Pond Island was the very island where John's father had taken the swarthy stranger! Indeed the fortune-teller told much which John knew was true!

Everyone had heard the story of how pirate Edward Low of Boston had buried treasure from the Spanish galleon *Don Pedro del Montclova* on Pond Island, but could it be a fact that after all the years that had intervened the treasure was still there awaiting someone to find it? It was incredible, but it also might be true.

Happy in his thoughts, John ran all the way down to Trefethen's Fish Wharf and scrambled into the dory. Nevertheless, there was one thing that worried him. Injun Bessie had warned him that neither he nor Ed would ever find the money alone, and he wanted to run the project. He realized that he didn't have the shrewdness Ed possessed, so how could he unite with the red-headed fisherman to get the gold? Ed would outwit him. For fully an hour John sat in the dory. The blazing sun shone down on him as he continued his pondering and scheming.

Finally Ed appeared. He had been with "friends from the city" and was in a talkative mood, but all his conversation failed to get a reply.

"What's the matter," jeered Ed, "haven't you found a way to break up a setting mackerel? I wonder if your system would work on fish."

"You were born on Pond Island, right?" asked John finally.

"You know I was."

"I just wanted to make sure." Neither spoke until Pumpkin Knob was left behind. Then John dropped a veritable bomb-shell.

"Ed, I'd give you a hundred dollars if you would go to Pond Island and dig for treasure with me!"

"There's only one trouble," came the answer. "You haven't got a hundred dollars. I know all about the treasure stories, but they are not true. Never mind, though, I'll go with you if we split fifty-fifty."

"No," answered John. "I'll raise what I give you to two hundred dollars. How about it?"

"Nothing doing, for it is half and half or nothing at all. Why are you so anxious not to pay me my fair share?"

"Well, today I have invested all my funds in the project, and I should realize something from the investment," concluded John.

The trip back home was completed in silence. There John decided to tell Ed the entire story, of his dream and of his interview with Injun Bessie. Ed observed that as he was born on the island, and regardless of John's dream and interview, they should split the gold in two. John's final remark was that he would give Ed five hundred dollars as his share, an offer that was immediately refused.

"These things are not always as simple as they seem," said Ed. "I was in the library in Portland the other month, and there was a story about pirates. One of them was hanged in Portland, up on Bramhall's Hill, at the guidepost where Backcove Road and Stroudwater Street came together. I don't want to be hanged."*

"You must be crazy. Finding pirate treasure doesn't mean that we get hanged," observed John.

Each man reached home. Neither told his wife much of anything, but for different reasons. Ed Green never did talk treasure tales over with his wife, while John Sylvester knew that if he suggested a partnership with Ed to his wife, he would be in for a tirade of sarcasm and ridicule that would end up with a prediction that he would be "neatly cheated by his slick colleague."

Ed did announce to his wife that "John is goin' digging for pirate gold on Pond Island," while John told Martha that he was thinking of going across to Pond Island to dig that very night. Martha did not object. As Williams Haynes suggests, she knew of no rich relatives in either branch of their family tree, so why not let him go across—he might be lucky!

And so it was that after dark John took pick, spade, gunny sack, and lantern, and went down to his punt to row across to Pond Island about a mile and a quarter from the beach where he lived. He chose a clump of trees near Will's Gut to get his

*See William Willis, *History of Portland*, pages 636–637. Hans Hanson and Thomas Bird had murdered the master of a small sloop of about thirty tons off the coast of Africa in 1789. They sailed into Casco Bay and "commenced a traffic with the inhabitants of Cape Elizabeth."

The naval commander of Portland then thought of capturing the sloop, but the pirates sailed away. Two vessels went out and found the sloop, which was brought into Portland Harbor on July 28, and the pirates were bound over for trial.

The two men were defended by John Frothingham and William Symmes. Englishman Bird was sentenced to be hanged and nineteen-year-old Hanson was acquitted by Judge Sewall. On the following June 25 the execution took place, with four thousand watching.

bearings, and rowed steadily until he landed on Pond Island beach.

About this time he began to wonder if the spirits of pirates might be around. Possibly Bessie had not told him everything about what might happen! He dragged his punt above the fringe of dried seaweed and gathered his tools together.

Concentrating on his dream, John tried to recall the exact part of the island where he had seen the squaw and a pirate in his dream lifting the cumbersome chest. He remembered that when Low, if it was Low, had concealed the treasure, it had been in a pond, and years later the pond had dried up. Already in the darkness he counted the outlines of four pits where four other groups had dug unsuccessfully for treasure; but his idea was to explore the southern shore carefully near a duck blind he had used some years ago during the hunting season. Although he swung the lantern carefully into every nook and cranny, nothing he saw resembled the area of his dream.

Just above the rocky shore was a part of the island where coarse grass and cedar trees grew. John decided to explore the area, which slanted downhill just a little into a hollow.

Suddenly he slipped, dislodging a boulder, which started a miniature landslide, and his lantern went out. Reaching to pick it up, he gave a yell of stark terror, for he saw a human skull, partly revealed by the landslide. Grabbing the lantern, he scrambled for his pick and spade, and was about to flee.

Suddenly he realized that here was what he was after, signs of pirates and possible treasure. Picking up the skull, he examined it carefully, and then placed it down on the ground some distance away. John wondered if he might be about to find what no one else had discovered, the gold of Edward Low.

Beginning to dig, John came across fragments of bone, pieces of crushed shells, and blackened lumps of what must originally have been links of chain.

Suddenly he hit a hard, unresisting object which gave an

ominous echo. As he raised his pick to strike again there came a deep, frightening groan, but just where the sound came from he could not tell. Bringing his pick down again, he heard another groan, blood-curdling in its intensity.*

Now he could trace the groan, for it was behind the rocks near where he had put down the skull. About to take his pick and crash through whatever he had hit before, he raised the tool slowly into the air. Then he heard a voice.

"Who's that digging for my gold?" came the unbelievable, terrifying words. John stood stunned for a moment, and then he made up his mind. Dropping everything, he scrambled out of the hollow and ran blindly for his punt. He tore through thickets and briars, falling again and again in his confusion and panic. Finally he reached the punt, which he pushed into the incoming tide. Soon he was rowing rapidly for Bailey Island.

Landing half an hour later, he abandoned the punt and ran for home. When he reached the top of the hill and burst into the house, he found his wife in the kitchen.

Martha took his excitement as a sign that he might have found the treasure, and asked him if he had been lucky.

"No, Martha, no! But I did have a terrible time." He sat down in the rocking chair, and after indulging in liquid refreshment, told her the entire story, omitting nothing.

In her wifely way, realizing that John really needed sympathy, Martha consoled him and soon he was fairly cheerful again. But the final blow was yet to come.

An hour later a knock sounded at the door. It was Ed Green. When he came in, he asked John how things were going. John said nothing, and then Ed wondered out loud if John might be willing to divide fifty-fifty now that he had had a longer time to think things over.

"I'm never going to Pond Island again," declared John, "and

*Writer Clara Louise Burnham of Illinois, 1854–1927, who summered at nearby Bailey Island, is said to be the source of this part of the Pond Island tale.

you can do what you wish about it."

"John has had a little trouble," interjected Martha. "Why don't you tell him, John?"

"What happened?"

"John seen a ghost!" explained Martha. "Over on Pond Island a few hours ago in the darkness."

"Yes, I did," offered John.

"I don't believe it," responded Ed. "Tell me about it."

John then told his story, beginning at the very moment when he landed his punt on Pond Island. He went through every single detail right up to his hurried return to Bailey Island. Ed followed the story, nodding and drinking in every word until the tale was finished.

"John," he began, "that does bear out everything Injun Bessie told you, doesn't it? Now if you and me went into partnership, for Injun Bessie said we couldn't find it alone, why we would both be rich! How about it?"

"I'm never going to set foot on Pond Island again," stated John, at which pledge Ed began to roar with laughter, and spoke up.

"You poor darn fool, that voice was me. I followed you over, saw your lantern, and began to spy on you. When you hit the plank or whatever it was, I groaned, and then groaned again. That is all it was, and you can forget it."

"No, Ed, it couldn't have been you. I know your voice."

"It was me all right, and you really was scared, believe me."

Ed left the unhappy couple shortly afterward, and then John and Martha talked things over. They finally agreed to go across to Pond Island someday when Ed was taking in another load of lobsters, and did so on the first calm day.

Arriving on the island, they found the place where John had been digging. They discovered the pick, and then found the shovel, but the lantern eluded them and they never found it. Looking into the hole he had dug, they were able to reach the hard substance which John's pick had struck that unusual night. It was a plank that evidently had been part of a shipwreck of many years before. They left Pond Island shortly after their discovery. There is an element of mystery about the skull, for they never found that object either.

As gifted Williams Haynes tells us in his version of the account, John never went "t'hunt fer no more pirate gold nowhere."

5

Buried Treasure

The Maine coast has been the scene of many treasure hunts. At Pond Island Boston pirate Edward Low is said to have buried his treasure, which he took from the Spanish galleon *Don Pedro del Montclova*. The treasure consisted of three kettles of bar silver and a large chest of gold and jewels.

Captain Low was said to have secreted the treasure in a pond on Pond Island, and then to have fled the vicinity. Later a mutiny ended the career of pirate Low. He was set adrift at sea and was seen no more. Thus he never came back to Pond Island to recover his loot.

During the last century, probably over a hundred expeditions have been sent out to Pond Island to look for the treasure, and as far as we know, the only person to profit thereby was the old hermit-king of the island, John Darling by name. Darling, whose diet consisted of periwinkles, clams, mussels, crabs, and an occasional fish, was the only resident of Pond Island around the turn of the century. It was said that the officials of Harpswell marooned him at Pond Island because he was constantly in trouble in town, but how much truth there was in this allegation has never been settled. Out on the island Darling lived in a tiny shack insulated with seaweed against the wintry cold, a shack he had built entirely of driftwood. The hermit was often hired to do the digging after the treasure seekers had chosen the location they felt was correct. Usually he would work for fifty cents a day, digging as deep a hole as his customers desired. But as far as is known, no one ever found Edward Low's treasure, although in places the island is pitted with the holes of treasure seekers. Darling died before the year 1928, and his shack was allowed to go to ruin.

Treasure of a strange type was the goal of a group of men who landed on Pond Island in 1801. They had been told by a stranger in Portland that he could extract silver from dew, and he said he would prove it. They all went out to Pond Island to test the theory. The first attempt failed. Another try was made, this time with the dew obtained "at the right time of the morning." The mysterious brew was heated, other ingredients were added, and surely enough, when the liquid cooled, several silver particles were found at the bottom of the container.

The group of men agreed to pay the stranger $250 apiece for the formula then and there, and the stranger vanished with the money. Of course, when the group attempted to produce silver again, they failed miserably, and soon realized that they had been duped by the "Acaraza Man," as he came to be called. Evidently the stranger had dropped the silver particles into the brew as he was stirring it.

During the War between the States a pot of gold was found on Haskell Island. The gold, plowed up by a farmer who then owned the island, was declared to be worth $1,800. Haskell Island, which we have visited by canoe, is just off Harpswell Neck, Maine.

*   *   *

At Harpswell Center, another farmer came across gold coins while he was plowing, and found that they were worth $1,100.

There is a small island in the Sassona River, near Bath, where a hidden treasure of unknown value was discovered in the last century. The details of the story, although known to the older inhabitants as late as 1900, are believed to have been lost forever.

Another unusual case of the finding of buried treasure concerns an aged Maine mother. On her deathbed she revealed to her son that her late husband had knowledge of a substantial treasure buried on Swan Island. The boy's father had long known of the existence of the treasure, but because he either was involved in its burial or knew something about the man who did bury it and realized that it was stolen money, he had always refused to touch the hoard. After the mother's death the son waited a respectable length of time and then journeyed out to Swan Island, located the treasure without too much difficulty, and realized a tidy sum from it. With the money he began a fish business, which later prospered.

PART FOUR

Canoe Trips, Excursions, and Special Islands

1

Our 1963 Canoe Trip

On eleven occasions I have paddled around Casco Bay in a canoe, making relatively long trips and exploring the many islands. Actually, it has been possible for me to land on every island that at one time or another has been inhabited. But there is a special overnight journey during the summer of 1963 that I'll never forget. I do not think that either Mrs. Snow or our daughter Dorothy will have much trouble recalling those delightful hours on that trip around the many isles of Casco Bay.

On Monday, August 12, 1963, we reached Orr's Island, which is located between the mainland and Bailey Island in Casco Bay, stopping at the store of S. J. Prince. After getting acquainted with Mr. Prince, we asked him about the Cob Bridge. It is built of granite blocks laid crosswise with spaces in between and had fascinated us ever since we first heard about it. Although many people think there is another bridge of this type in Europe, that assumption is not true. This is the only cob bridge of its kind in the world. He explained that before the bridge had been put up between Orr's Island and Bailey Island in 1928, a steamboat would come up to the wharf at Orr's

Island with passengers and supplies.

The old wharf was about a thousand yards from Prince's store, which had been started by his grandfather, Gushing Prince, many years before. Mr. S. J. Prince explained to us that the Prince family had been on the island for 116 years.

We went over to the Cob Bridge, and Dorothy and my wife, Anna-Myrle, spent some time climbing in and out of the huge granite blocks. After taking pictures of the two at the bridge, I walked with them back to our car, which had the canoe on top for our long trip around Casco Bay.

We drove across the Cob Bridge and sped up hill and down dale until we arrived at the Bailey Island pier. Here there was a tremendous amount of activity. We met and talked with Corinne Merrill, who lived in the yellow and white house we had passed before reaching the tidal waters below. She told us of the interesting people in the vicinity who would have local knowledge of Bailey Island, and mentioned in particular Helen Murray, Linwood Johnson, and Philip Johnson.

There had been fair weather that morning, but it soon started to rain moderately hard. We ate a delicious lobster-salad sandwich while we talked with Corinne about our journey, and she gave us many tips of importance. Then we loaded our dunnage, life preservers, and supplies aboard our canoe.

At 3:24 that afternoon, with Dorothy resting amidships and Anna-Myrle in the position of bow paddler, I pushed the canoe off the shale and slid over into the stern seat. We were ready for our trip of history, romance, and adventure around Casco Bay.

Corinne Merrill waved farewell to us as we entered the outer area of Bailey Island's Mackerel Cove. On our right as we paddled we went by a little cavern in the high rocky ledge that reached thirty or forty feet above us. Then came a more spectacular indentation, which did not develop into a cave as we hoped, but turned out to be merely a break in the ledge wall.

A third cavern looked like a giant canyon and there was what resembled a huge natural tombstone at the right.

Leaving the protection of Mackerel Cove, we entered the unsheltered depths off the Maine coast. Quite some distance ahead we noticed what appeared to be a large vessel whose sails gave an indication of an ancient ship apparently resembling the *Mayflower* coming toward us. When the craft drew alongside, she proved to be a much smaller vessel than we had believed, carrying a very unusual diamond-shaped sail. Although we waved to the occupants hoping they would slow up so we could inspect the sail, we were ignored. They showed no interest in our efforts, and soon were but a speck in the distance.

Shortly afterward the Casco Bay Lines boat *Nellie G., III*, which had left Custom House Wharf in Portland at two o'clock on her regular run, came up alongside us. The captain waved, and of course we responded. Soon after this a sleek cabin cruiser went by, cutting the water at great speed, the spray carrying entirely over her. Next a fishing boat passed us and we waved in answer to the helmsman's greeting.

A short time later a friendly porpoise came along, jauntily broaching the surface every minute or so. Dorothy immediately thought of Flipper, the principal actor in a current television show. Our friend was a much smaller edition and considerably darker in color.

On the starboard side we approached in gradual fashion a headland which I believed was part of Haskell Island, and then we debated whether the island in the distance might be Jewel Island, although it was far away. A little tower on the nearby island on the right intrigued us. Was it a marker or a summer house, and did it at one time have a light on top? I believe it was octagonal in shape. Then we noticed off to the left a thin black and white pyramid on a relatively small island which I recognized as Little Mark Island. Double-crested cormorants flying astern of the canoe caused us to wonder if they nested nearby. I dipped my toes into the water contemplating a swim. It didn't seem too cold to take a plunge, but I decided not to go in at the moment.

Several sailboats were heeled over in the afternoon breeze, their occupants suitably attired in bright-colored oilskins. Far astern of us the clouds began to pile up like fluffy whipped cream. One sailing craft then rounded what we later learned was Great Mark Island. The surf began to pound high on Haskell Island as we approached the shore, and so we decided not to land there at that time.

Then Dorothy told us that at 11:25 that morning she had seen a UFO, silver-colored, going faster than a jet. She had waited to tell us about it in the canoe, as she did not want to mention it at the time she saw the strange object. It seemed too improbable.

At 4:30 P.M. we noticed two men in an outboard motorboat fishing at anchor off Haskell Island. Coming alongside, we found they were Matthew Herrold, a lawyer, and Don Wilson, a business consultant.

"The fishing is not good at all," one of them told us.

We then approached close to Great Mark Island and were hopeful of finding a place to land. Great Mark is situated between Haskell Island and Little Mark Island, which is the location of the pyramid that had attracted our attention earlier.

As we paddled our canoe toward Great Mark, the boat with the two fishermen passed by and landed on the beach ahead of us. After we jumped out of the canoe and pulled it up beyond the reach of the tide, we stretched to relieve our muscles and then climbed over the rocks to explore the usually uninhabited island. Dorothy observed some red berries, and we discovered that they were wild raspberries just coming into season. Eventually we managed to find several hundred on the bushes above the rocks.

While we were picking the berries, there was a sudden shout

from above us. I looked at the two agitated fishermen and then turned around and saw their motorboat drifting off to sea. We had pulled our canoe up above the reach of the tide, but they had not been quite so careful. Scrambling down to the shore, I waded into the water to grab the painter just as the motorboat slipped around the rocks and started out. Retrieving the boat, I pulled it in toward shore as one of the men reached the scene. I gave him the line, which he took rather sheepishly, and a few minutes later the fishermen pushed off. Soon they were "hull down."

Ten minutes later we found a delightful pulpit rock about twenty-five feet high on the Haskell Island side of Mark Island.

Returning to the canoe, we ate our lunch, had the raspberries for dessert, and then rested a while before leaving the island. It was then around 5:45. As we paddled along we noticed that the old-fashioned lobster buoys had much longer sticks in Casco Bay than in Boston Harbor, where we have canoed for half a century. We also learned that plastic Clorox bottles and the like were revolutionizing the lobster business, because the lobstermen make buoys and floats out of them. I am told that all such containers, no matter what label they bear, are suitable for this activity. They are also trimmed and used for bailing.

We paddled toward the sun, then getting lower in the west, and set our course in the direction of Eagle Island, which I believed to be Admiral Peary's home. We were eager to visit the island where Peary made plans for his successful discovery of the North Pole on April 6, 1909.

It was now getting very rough, with waves breaking into the canoe, some sliding up over the gunwales. Bailing became necessary. At six o'clock we were still paddling into the sun, less than an eighth of a mile off Admiral Peary's island.

Within a few moments we found that Eagle Island was inhabited, and several of the residents were in sight. A large white house, gleaming in the late afternoon sun, was built up over the headland, with a castle motif of Gothic or Norman masonry below it. We noticed a seal playing around the rocks, and sandpipers along the shore, all lined up facing the wind.

Two men and a woman came out on the plateau above the masonry and waved us in to visit. One man stood on the parapet and watched us as we came along. We decided not to risk sliding onto the bar that went out from the island, as the sea surges might have succeeded in capsizing us. A short distance away I saw a relatively quiet cove where a pier had been built many years ago. We landed there and met the two men, caretakers of the house, both of whom, we discovered, were Bowdoin College graduates of the Class of 1963. Bill Kruse of Wilmington, Delaware, commuted from the Casco Bay mainland to the island and back by means of an outboard skiff. His partner, John Meader of Meaderville, Maine, distinguished himself by wearing a full beard.

They took us up to the house on the plateau, where Marie Harte Stafford, wife of Commander Edward Stafford, the author of the book *The Big E*, greeted us. She introduced the other members of the family, including a great grandson of Admiral Peary, and showed us through the house where the admiral had planned so many of his expeditions. We were particularly interested in her story of Admiral Peary's daughter, Marie Peary Stafford, known as the Snow Baby, who was born north of the Arctic Circle. At the time of our visit she was living in Brunswick, Maine.

Our hostess was called Ree. She told us her address was Eagle Island, South Harpswell, Maine. Mrs. Stafford graciously took us around the island, and we were fascinated by the tour.

Then came the moment of farewell, and Dorothy took the bow paddle from Anna-Myrle.

Our next objective was Bates Island, the home of Arnold Wald, whose off-island residence was usually Portchester, New York. Bates Island, we were informed, was owned by John Rich of the National Broadcasting Company. We met Arnold Wald and his wife Edith on the island, and they introduced us to their seven children: Kathy, nine; Adrienne, eight; Richard, seven; Lois, five; Donald, four; David, one year and four months; and Elizabeth, three months. There were two nieces with them, Alice Prince and Barbara Johansen. The powerful basset hound, Moe, which appeared to be four feet long and was seemingly built in sections, was the final member of the complement on Bates Island.

After a short visit, for the sun was setting, we resumed our journey, heading for Cliff Island. Paddling almost directly into a fiercely red sun, we found ourselves in the area between Cliff and Hope Islands. And twenty minutes later, with the last glow vanishing and the utter blackness of night beginning to take its place, I sighted a tiny spark of illumination that could be nothing other than a light from a cottage on Cliff Island.

Soon we neared the island's rocky shore. I flashed my light on a landing that revealed the title Scuttlebutt. I then noticed, even in the darkness, bright orange steps almost glowing in the gloom at one of the island's various piers.

At 8:50, weary but somewhat revived with a sense of anticipation, we arrived at the landing of Dr. and Johanna von Tiling. We had met Johanna many years before on the ferry because of a misunderstanding over our briefcases. As soon as we touched the beach I called out in a loud voice. We pulled the canoe up out of the reach of the tide, and I went ahead, climbing the flagstone steps made of natural rock that led up to the von Tiling residence high above the shore. There I found that Johanna had been aroused by my call and was already dressing to greet us. She and her father, Dr. Johannes von Tiling, were very excited, indeed almost unbelieving, that we had arrived in the dark and had come out of the night by canoe. Johanna cried out that she must go down to the shore to see Anna-Myrle and Dorothy. Running down the steps, she went across the road and out onto the rocky beach, where she greeted the other two members of the party.

After the excitement of the unexpected arrival had died down, Johanna brought us up to date on a plane crash that had occurred just off Cliff Island the month before.

On July 7, at about ten at night, Johanna had answered a phone call from Westbrook, Maine. "It was a girl musically associated with me," she said. "The girl told me there was a plane down near Cliff Island. I tried to call several locations on the island to discover details, but apparently everyone had gone out to the scene of the wreck. Then I telephoned a local radio station and they said that all they knew was that a plane was down near Cliff Island. A moment later the coast guard called me and asked the following question, 'What have you done with the four people who have gone ashore?'

"It was Commander Kenneth Outen of the South Portland Base, and I had to tell him that I had no knowledge of anyone's coming ashore as yet, but I would find out as soon as I could. Actually, as I learned later, the plane had gone down at the south end of the island, about a hundred and fifty yards offshore. The four men aboard, a Mr. Cahner, his two sons and the pilot, had been able to swim the hundred and fifty yards to safety ashore."

After Johanna had given us the details of the crash, we told her of our own adventures. We planned to visit no less than ten islands on our trip, which would end the next day. After a delightful meal, we were given "lodging for the night" and were soon asleep.

Early in the morning after a hearty breakfast we were down on the beach packing the canoe for the second day of our journey. Our immediate destination was Hope Island. After pushing away from Cliff Island and waving farewell to Johanna and Dr. von Tiling, we made good progress, landing about twenty minutes later at low tide relatively close to the flagpole

at Hope Island. It had begun to rain. We clambered up the steep
rocky incline and met the ladies at the great house high above
the beach. They told us the total number then staying at the
island included the following: Mr. and Mrs. Samuel A. Breene,
Mr. and Mrs. David G. Leach, Mr. and Mrs. Leo M. Brewster,
Mrs. Virginia R. Rhoads, Mr. and Mrs. Herbert A. C. Rauchfuss, and Mr. and Mrs. Thomas McConnell.

The ladies explained that all of the menfolk had just left for
the mainland. The group were members of what was known as
the Hope Island Club, and they received their mail at the Cliff
Island Post Office.

Mrs. Rauchfuss loaned me a history of Hope Island and
Casco Bay which her husband had written in 1959. The forty-
two-page book was delightful and takes the reader back to
around the year 1600, when the Abenaki Indians went out to
the islands on various occasions.

In the large comfortable living room of the great house, a
stuffed owl named Ginsburg attracted our attention. The focal
point of the room, however, was a grand fireplace over which
were written the words:

YE ARE ALL WELCOME AND THE HEARTH
GROWS BRIGHTER WITH THE JOY OF YOUR PRESENCE.

Soon after our departure from Hope Island, the rain became
a pelting downpour, and from its steadily developing crescendo
we knew we were about to be assaulted more harshly by the
elements. Little cat's-paws of wind could be seen all around us.
Whenever a squall struck, we braced ourselves, and I steadied
the canoe with my paddle. Every so often we watched fascinated as areas of increasingly heavy rain, veritable sheets,
approached our canoe. At first the drops made a pattering
sound as they struck the water, but as the heavy squall drew
closer there was a drumming of overpowering intensity. Soon

we were in the middle of the storm, and the tattoo resembled a barrage. Then all of a sudden it was gone, replaced by a relatively steady but quiet downpour.

We touched at Rogue's Island and then at Sand Island. The houses of Great Chebeague were visible off to our left. We paused only briefly at Chebeague, failing even to get a glimpse of the lone oak, for it was on the other side of the island.

In fairly rapid succession we touched at Little Bangs, Stave Island, Ministerial, and Stockman, but the rain did not inspire us. We decided to make an effort to reach the monument on Little Mark Island, built back in 1827 as a refuge for ship-wrecked sailors, or if that was not possible, to give up our goal and merely land at Haskell Island.

As we passed Eagle Island the waves did not seem too high, so we agreed to make a final try for Mark, an effort that resulted in success. Just as the low tide began to turn, we found a delightful but small rocky canal at Little Mark Island into which we steered the canoe.

Soon we touched shore and pulled the canoe high above any venturesome wave or the reach of the incoming tide, making the craft safe for the next hour. Anna-Myrle and Dorothy went ahead to reach the monument as I decided to pull the canoe even higher. Finally, for complete safety, I tied the canoe to a paddle and forced the paddle into the crevice of a ledge.

By the time I had secured the canoe's line to the paddle both Dorothy and Anna-Myrle were out of sight. The island, proba-bly little more than an acre in size and very steep, resembles Egg Rock off Nahant, Massachusetts, except that it seems to have more foliage and grass above the rocks.

When I caught up with my wife and daughter at the foot of the monument, they had already inspected the Mariner's Ref-uge, as it was called, a dismal dungeon inside the base of the tower. The ceiling of the dungeon was no more than four or five feet high. Its present use is to store the batteries and other necessary equipment to run the light at the top of the monument. The tall, black and white granite edifice rises seventy-four feet above the sea, and the light flashes every four seconds.

Mrs. Snow and Dorothy, the latter a little reluctantly, climbed the iron ladder that was spiked to the granite pyramid. I stayed behind, figuring that discretion was the better part of valor, for one or two of the lower rungs didn't seem too strong and might give way under my 216 pounds. The ladies had no trouble, and each in turn waved to me from the top.

After photographing this adventure, we walked around the island, but with the weather as it was, my chief concern was getting away from this lonely marine outpost as soon as possible. I sent Dorothy down over the brow of the hill to check on the canoe, and she shouted back that all was well. Ten minutes later we had reached our craft and were backing out of that delightfully located, low-tide rocky canal.

When we had been walking around the island we had noticed a group fishing in a small outboard motorboat. When they saw us getting ready to leave in the canoe, for some reason they hastily pulled anchor and motored away from us.

It was now time to think about the weather again. Ominous darker clouds were gathering all around us. Off to sea we noticed a great fog bank starting in. Since approaching fog has never filled me with confidence, we decided to head right for Bailey Island and end our voyage there. Nevertheless, as sometimes happens, after two minutes of paddling our courage rose again, and we agreed we might consider going around the tip of Haskell Island to see if there was a suitable landing place. There might be an island resident we could interview as well.

Half an hour later we came up to the beach on Haskell Island, passing an empty anchored seiner piled high with nets. Immediately ahead of us was a red farmhouse. Off to the left over a ledge was a white house, possibly a summer resident's home. We landed on the beach just ahead of the incoming tide, and

I secured the canoe by tying the line around a fifteen-pound boulder.

Since we had noticed smoke coming out of the chimney of the white house, we decided to call there. I gave several halloos and finally a lady appeared. She was probably dubious as to what we were doing in the area. When I brought up Anna-Myrle and Dorothy and explained that we were canoeing around Casco Bay, she invited us in. Her name was Mrs. James Noyes. Mrs. Noyes told us she came to the island in 1932 because its beauty and isolation attracted her.

Mrs. Noyes said that the red house was owned by the Little family, and that if I wanted to know more about it I should interview Mrs. Charles Baker of Newburyport, Massachusetts. Mrs. Baker was the daughter of Mr. Little, and when she was on the island she lived in the red house, one of the oldest in all Maine.*

We enjoyed a fine meal at Mrs. Noyes' residence. I especially remember the freshly baked cake with chocolate frosting she had for us.

Finally the time for departure came. The rain had neither stopped nor held off. Unknown to us, a very bad storm was rapidly approaching, but as we were on the lee side of the island, it didn't hurt us at all until we paddled out to face the relatively choppy seas.

After a few minutes of canoeing, we looked up to see again the unusual edifice at Haskell Island which is probably octagonal in shape. It looked like a lighthouse, but Mrs. Baker later told us it had never been used except as an ornamental beacon. It is probably about fifteen or eighteen feet in diameter and on the roof is what I believe Mrs. Baker stated was a bell tower.

*When I talked with Mrs. Baker later, she said, "I remember when I was a small girl seeing an Indian paddle across from Potts Harbor to Mackerel Cove. He stood up in a rather rough sea all the time. I was told later that they always paddled standing up unless there was some special reason to do otherwise."

She said that it had been brought out from the mainland by one of the earlier owners.

Forty-five minutes later we landed back at our starting point at Bailey Island. The rain was still coming down, but we managed to get the canoe back atop our car and were soon leaving Casco Bay for our Marshfield home. Our trip of adventure was over.

2

Cliff Island and Long Island

In 1916, writing in his delightful volume *Casco Bay Yarns*, the late Williams Haynes of Aucocisco, Cliff Island, said that his interest in the area began when he went out early one morning in 1911 to help "haul a line of lobster pots."

My own interest in Casco Bay definitely started because of a misunderstanding between one of our party and Miss Johanna von Tiling aboard the Casco Bay craft approaching Cliff Island. After the confusion (because of a similarity in briefcases) was quickly straightened out, we accepted an invitation to visit Cliff Island. The warm welcome by Dr. and Miss von Tiling and the other islanders drew us back to Casco Bay time and time again.

Cliff Island really combines all that an island should be, being insular in both character and personality, with the necessities of the big city available not too far away. It seems to be a town within itself, possibly because it is farther out than other inhabited areas in Casco Bay which have any sort of real population. It combines pine forests, rocky coves and inlets, beautiful hills, valleys, meadows and sandy beaches. Two miles long, the main part of the island is approximately a quarter mile in width for the most part.

When Dr. Johannes von Tiling brought his wife and daughter to Cliff Island in the summer of 1914 he found the island ideally suited to his dream of tranquility and rest, for there were no electric cars, no telephones and no bustling highways. Cliff Island was entirely free from many of the unfortunate circumstances that accompany what civilization has inflicted on its human creatures. The doctor found the island was a peaceful haven for the artist, lawyer, physician, scholar and musician. It offered him generously what might be called a Victorian atmosphere, completely unsullied and as yet unmarked by the mainland activities of people who have little consideration for the rights of others.

And so it was that Dr. von Tiling established himself on Cliff Island, where he was to spend most of the remaining part of his long life.

Almost every ancient map of the area titles the island Crotch, but the residents do not accept Crotch and prefer Cliff. The present identification of Cliff goes back to agitation led by Asher Black. Asher was a go-getter, and using the fact that there was already a Crotch Island Post Office in another Maine area, won out, and Cliff Island it is today.

When flying in from Halfway Rock toward Portland, the shape of Cliff Island reminds me of a cannon facing Cape Elizabeth. Others believe the letter H is also suggested. Viewed from the air, the island presents on its seaward side a cluster of wharves and fishing buildings used by the industrious residents of the island who seek their living from Casco Bay waters. Cod, haddock, and flounder are caught, with shrimp and scallops a bonus to the fishermen. Lobstering, of course, is more important than anything else.

We were very grateful several years ago when a lobsterman from the MacVane family brought us all the distance back to Portland at the time the regular boat did not run.

The names of early owners at Cliff Island include Chadwick

and Higgins. It is said that Abijal Chadwick, a resident of Beverly, Massachusetts, demanded that Benjamin Higgins be forced to move from his illegal residence on Cliff Island. Higgins had settled on several Cliff Island acres without permission. Chadwick stated that his mother, Eleanor Dundas, had owned the island, to which Higgins had no right. According to historian Herbert Jones, Chadwick won his case.

The island census for 1832 reveals that there were six families living on Cliff Island, all of them making their living from the sea.

A century ago the fishermen and boatbuilders of Crotch Island developed their own style of craft, a Crotch Island pinky, and soon other fishermen from other islands were anxious to have one of the new boats. The early name of the island is preserved in the Crotch Island pinky, with the unusual spritsail that makes it easily identifiable. Although these fishing craft became famous up and down the Maine coast by the turn of the century, shipbuilding on the island today isn't nearly what it was at the outbreak of World War II.

Association Hall is an important building at Cliff Island. During the year many functions are enjoyed at the hall, and it has been my pleasure to lecture there on several occasions. Musical programs are given from time to time, and both residents and off-islanders get together for dinners and other programs of mutual interest. Built in the year 1949, the Association Hall was constructed with lumber which came from World War II barracks at House Island. All work was done voluntarily, with the workers donating not only their time but often their money when additional funds were needed.

The island today has about eighty winter residents, with the number swelling to four hundred in the summer season.

On the western side of Cliff Island is the Casco Bay pier, where the Portland boat lands on a regular schedule. For the captains of the Casco Bay Lines craft, during that part of the year when Bailey is not the terminal, Cliff Island is the "end of the line." It is the closest the boat comes toward Halfway Rock Lighthouse. Summer and winter, as the motor vessel approaches the pier, we look forward to seeing the well-known figure and personality Miss Johanna von Tiling, waving a greeting to us. Leider singer and schoolteacher, she came to the island just before Williams Haynes wrote his book.

Near the pier is the flagpole, which can be seen for quite some distance, and the tennis court is next to Association Hall in a prominent position. Many of the winter and summer residences, with their own gardens, private landings, and delightful walks, are also on this side of the island. Some distance down the road to the left is the relatively small but still impressive cemetery where we often find small offerings of wild flowers in front of some of the gravestones.

On the eastern side of the main part of the island is the busy little one-room school building with its displays of colorful cutouts of the lower grades as well as the older classes' reading and writing assignments on the blackboards. Next to the school is a church conducted by members of the Seventh Day Adventist denomination, which holds services on Saturdays.

This was formerly an area of shipbuilding. Lobster pots and buoys are in evidence, still reminding the visitor of the maritime aspect of the island.

The post office, an attractive building, has an elevated walk with a fenced railing to the entrance.

There are differences of opinion as to the name of the first resident of Cliff Island. Hannah Small, the daughter of Uncle Sam Pettengill, as he was called, probably lived (at one time) in the oldest house. When Herbert Jones visited the island he discovered that the house had been built of hand-hewn wooden planks stood on end, in contrast to the usual horizontal manner of building. Author Jones learned that the house was constructed by John Merriman, who may have been the island's earliest resident. Called a piggin house, this type of building never was too popular in Maine, some say because of its intricate design. Another piggin is said to have been built at Kittery Point in 1630.

It is believed that Crotch or Cliff Island was first used by Parson Jonathan Flint for the pasturing of cows, but the parson never lived on the island as far as is known.

In 1768 Samuel Dean paid twelve pounds and ten shillings for property at Cliff Island. A Captain Larrabee had the island named for him at one time, as he owned a goodly part of it, while such titles as Dutch Island, the Nubble, Crow Island, and Parson Seabury's Island all have relationship with Cliff Island as we know it today.

Mrs. Doris Olney tells us in her delightful *Cliff Island Notebook* that there were in the year 1886 nine owners of property at Cliff Island: David Griffin, Hannah Small, Charles Griffin, Samuel, Charles, Nathaniel, and Moses Pettengill, Alpheus Griffin, and Benjamin Hammond.

The oldest house now standing on the island is believed by some to be that called Hannah Small's, the white saltbox residence on the "edge of Fisherman's Cove just beyond the little road which goes to Fisherman's Wharf." Until 1913, the Henry Griffin residence was the oldest on the island, but it was destroyed by fire that year. Another residence, on the South Point, was formerly owned by the Griffin family. It is claimed by some to be the oldest house, but disputes of this type are hard to settle.

In the year 1907 the island library was founded by Mrs. Louella Stone, who served there faithfully for twenty-three years. Johanna von Tiling was librarian after that for nine years, and is still an important member of the library group today.

Quite often I fly over Cliff Island to drop my Flying Santa

gifts from the air. Once in a while the packages are not immediately found. In 1966 I dropped four bundles from the airplane and only three turned up. The searchers were quite disappointed when they learned I had released four over the island, but after a few months even the most avid hunter gave up. Almost three years went by. Then, in August, 1969, a summer resident made a discovery. Daniel Hunting went out to his tool shed and for the first time noticed a hole in the roof of the building. Investigating, Hunting found my package, which had lain on the floor ever since the drop of December, 1966.

Apparently Cliff Island has a special fountain of youth, for one of her long-time residents, famed artist Norman Black, has just reached the age of ninety-one.

Schoolteaching is of vital importance on islands offshore along the Maine coast. Although I taught school for a generation, I do not think that I would have the fortitude to handle all the classes of an eight-grade curriculum in one room as is necessary on Cliff Island and many other islands of the Maine coast.

The respect of all readers who have taught school should be given to the following teachers who have labored at Cliff Island: Leila Searles, Phyllis Brown, Althea Cushing McKinney, Frances Barrett, Amanda Hinds, Dorothy Hatt, Virginia Norris, Catherine Anderson, Mary Messinger, Vera Mitchell, Sandra Meyerowitz, and Johanna von Tiling. The one-room school on Cliff Island is an important part of the Portland system.

Without question, Long Island can be considered the center of a group of islands of the outer bay, with Peak's to the southwest, Great Diamond to the west, Hope to the northeast, Chebeague to the north, and Cliff across Luckse Sound to the east.

The original name was Lange Eylande. The actual owners

were Sir Ferndinado Gorges and Captain John Mason.

Long Island to me will always be the isle where a clam bake was held that would have stretched through a solid mile of picnic tables if they had been arranged in a straight line! Held in 1886, this monster bake burned eleven cords of wood and set a record for all Casco Bay.

More than a hundred years earlier Colonel Ezekiel Cushing himself had started the tradition of the Casco Bay clam boil, in which clams are boiled like lobsters rather than baked. Cushing had his guests sip the clam broth from giant sea-clam shells as they ate the steamed bivalves. They often recited the thought quoted below:

> Clams are perfect the year all through
> Come, eat my clams, bid the doctor adieu.

Several generations later the large hotels were built, almost each of which had a steamboat landing. Cushing Landing, Cleaves Landing, Ponce Landing and Doughty's Landing were important wharves, with three hotels called Cushing House, Granite Spring Hotel, and the Dirigo House. All are gone today, and visitors often stay at several of the 286 homes on the island.

Possibly the best-known Long Island shipwreck was the loss of the schooner *Ada Barker,* which crashed at Junk of Pork, a small isle close to Outer Green Island. When the Long Island fishermen reached the wreck, the survivors had salvaged the wreckage and were making the best of their situation on the lonely ledge two miles from Long Island.

Long Island's northeasterly end was taken over by the Navy in World War II, and a submarine net was put in between Long Island and Chebeague. Various craft were sunk in the area to make the blockade more successful.

The old days of giant clam bakes and boils, band concerts,

and dance orchestras may be gone forever, replaced by radios, television, and telephones. Nevertheless, it is still possible to land at Long Island today and in the coming years and return to the generations of long ago, when the relative isolation of Long Islanders was more apparent.

3

Chebeague Island

Great Chebeague Island is one of the largest islands in the Casco Bay area. The early charts often call the island Chebidisco, meaning in the Indian language the isle of many springs. Perhaps the Indians enjoyed their visits to Chebeague more than those to any other island, for even today there are gigantic heaps of historic and prehistoric shells, and once in a while broken tomahawks and pestles are found in the debris.

It was the custom for generations of red men from all over Maine and even Canada to choose the moon that includes June for their visits to Chebeague. The spectacle of myriads of Indian birch bark canoes pulling up on the shores of the island must indeed have been an inspiring sight. While ashore they busied themselves with fishing, drying the fish for winter consumption, and even capturing seals and whales. They mastered the art of preserving clams and mussels for the long months ahead, and they hunted the porpoise, whose skin they used in making snowshoes.

The Indians chose the same general clearings that later were occupied by the early white settlers, setting up their wigwams for the week's festive reunions. There they would celebrate with sports, lacrosse especially, and carry out their dances, which were always accompanied by songs.

Some say that a frequent visitor to Chebeague Island was the Great Spirit Glooskap, the so-called pleasure-loving demigod, who was anxious to keep the Indians away from the clutches of Granny Squannit, otherwise known as the witch woman or the sea woman.

I'll never forget the tale told me concerning Granny.* It seems she was very influential in getting the whales to come close to shore so that the Indians could capture them. One day as Granny was mending a tear in Glooskap's cap, she pricked her finger. When the wound began to bleed, she demanded a drop of blood from the finger of Glooskap. He gave her what she asked, but the ruby drop missed her finger and fell to the bottom of the marsh. A second drop of Glooskap's blood was demanded. This touched Granny's finger and healed the wound.

Glooskap then fell asleep, and the sea woman made her way down to the shores of Chebeague. There on the beach, facing Seguin, she sang the song of the whales. Out on the ocean the whales heard the song and were said to have been quite surprised. Glooskap awakened with a start, astounded at what was happening. Meanwhile, the clams, for it was low tide, joined in the chorus, singing alto, to the accompaniment of the whales singing bass. Glooskap also began to sing, and his giant tenor voice really shook the surrounding hills and valleys.

The song ended and Glooskap again grew drowsy, but the sea woman persisted in keeping him awake, for she wanted just one puff on his pipe of peace. He granted her wish, she took a long puff, and then she sat back, contented.

"There's just one more favor, O Glooskap, and if you will

*Since hearing the tale I have discovered that ninety years ago Charles G. Leland told a slightly different version in his authoritative *Algonquin Legends of New England.*

grant it, I'll make all the red men happy."

"What is that favor?" asked Glooskap.

"Present me with the pipe you have which you never use, and I'll give you a whale for your worshippers, the Indians."

Glooskap presented the sea woman with his spare pipe, and she lighted it and enjoyed a long, comfortable smoke.

"Don't forget your promise," admonished Glooskap.

"That I will never do," came the reply, and the sea woman went across to the headland where she could see the whales frolicking. Awaiting high tide, she watched the great creatures cavorting in the water just offshore. Kneeling down on the beach, the sea woman witch put her mouth into the water and sucked the salty brine in, whence the tide went out, leaving a great whale stranded on the beach. The Indians were very pleased and used the whale to advantage within a few hours.

The sea woman is said to have perished when all the other women on the island, who hated her, combined to entomb her in a cave on the western side of the island.

The dance in memory of the sea woman was perhaps the best of all the dances the Indians performed when they enjoyed their June week on the island. Early in the morning they would go to the sea woman's walled-up cave and put special food on a stone altar.

When the sun rose, ceremonial dances would begin in the sea woman's honor. Indian warriors with brightly painted faces formed two long lines, their turkey feathers waving in the wind. The medicine drums began to beat, slowly at first, then faster and faster. As the dance went on, one by one the red men faltered from exhaustion, stepping out of the dance and waiting for the last dancer who would win the contest. Incidentally, the squaws never joined in this particular dance, for they hated the sea woman, who had often stolen their braves.

This Indian legend and several others were told to me by a well-known resident of Chebeague, whose only wish was that she remain unmentioned in this book. She emphasized her desire for anonymity.

It is said by some that even the great Madockawando, whose daughter Mathilde married Baron Castin in 1687, visited Chebeague Island on several occasions, and that his friendship prevented the Indians from becoming belligerent toward the white settlers on the island.*

Even during the terrible massacres of whites by the Indians throughout many communities of southern Maine, Chebeague's white settlers lived side by side as equals with the Indians.

One day on the island an obviously intoxicated Indian brave was heard approaching the home of a Chebeague settler. All were away fishing except two women who hastily barred the door. Knocking loudly, the Indian demanded rum, while the two women cringed inside.

A moment later came the shrill cry of an Indian squaw whom the two watchers saw approach the brave with a club. She clouted the red man and gave him a sound thrashing, after which the brave, who was her son, slouched off into the woods in meekness and shame.

The first proprietor of Chebeague was a royal personage, none other than Sir Ferdinando Gorges. It was not until 1650, however, that Chebeague Island is mentioned on a legal document. This was written by a deputy of Gorges' to a Bostonian named Merry.

Great Chebeague Island contains more than two thousand acres. When granted by George Cleeve to Walter Merry on September 18, 1650, it became known as Merry's Island. It is not known whether or not he ever visited the island, but Merry sold it to a John King for five hundred pounds. Then on October 8, 1675, the island was conveyed by Robert Canton in New Plymouth to Josiah Willes of Boston.

*See my *Strange Tales* from Nova Scotia to Cape Hatteras, pps 85–89.

After King Philip's War, Indian fighter Walter Gendall became interested in Chebeague Island. On July 12, 1680, he bought 650 acres on the eastern side of the island. Upon his death, around the year 1700, his administrator, Theodosius Moore, married Gendall's widow.

Before that date, however, in 1683, Massachusetts granted Richard Wharton 650 acres on the western side of Chebiscodego, as Chebeague was then known. In turn his administrator, Ephraim Savage, conveyed the island to the deacons of Boston's First Church for the use of the poor, calling the isle Recompense Island, a name that did not last long.

In 1743 part of the island was bought by Colonel Thomas Westbrook, the King's Royal Mast Agent. Westbrook built the first bridge across Fore River, and Westbrook, Maine, is named for him.

In 1760 a Scot named Ambrose Hamilton purchased a segment of the island for farming. Many have called Hamilton Chebeague's first citizen. He constructed a log cabin on the north shore. After he married he had twelve children and lived to enjoy seventy-one grandchildren. There are many Hamilton descendants living on Chebeague today.

Ebenezer Hill appeared at Chebeague sometime late in the eighteenth century. Although no members of the Hill family were mentioned in the list of participants in the Boston Tea Party, his father is said to have been one of those dressed in Indian costumes who threw the tea into Boston Harbor. In any case, Ebenezer built a brick dwelling from clay he baked on the shore. Later, as captain of an American vessel, he was made a prisoner by a British frigate and imprisoned at Bermuda for a year, confined on the same island where Stephen Decatur was incarcerated.

Decatur* had been captured after his proud warship *Presi-*

*See Sister Jean de Chantel Kennedy, *Biography of a Colonial Town*, pages 105–107, for more details.

dent first got into trouble by running aground in the fog on a sandbar off Sandy Hook, New Jersey. When the *President*'s copper plating was ripped off, the ship began to leak. Two hours later Decatur managed to free the *President*, but the fog, which would have allowed him to escape, then lifted, revealing four British warships.

And so it was that on January 15, 1815, the last battle ever fought between England and America took place between the *Endymion* and the *President*. Although the *Endymion* was overwhelmed, the *President* had no chance of eventual victory, and Decatur had to surrender.

It was not Decatur's proudest moment. He and his men were taken to Bermuda aboard the *Endymion*. While he was in St. George, Decatur, who was slightly wounded, talked with Chebeague Island's Ebenezer Hill, and Hill never forgot it.

The name of Ellis Ames Ballard, whose summer home, Khatmandu, is indeed a showplace, should always be remembered when Chebeague is mentioned. When we visited his grounds some years ago the members of his family were more than generous, and opened their bathhouse for us down near the tall oak tree which can be seen from almost anywhere in the area. Ellis Ames Ballard is responsible for the excellent baseball diamond at Chebeague, as well as the unusual golf course, which has within its area a tiny picturesque cemetery sketched by Herbert G. Jones in the year 1945.

The Chebeague Island stone sloops will forever occupy an important place in Maine history. Z. William Hauk was an avid collector of pictures and information about the stone sloops, and his book on the subject is a masterpiece. It was my privilege during the brief interlude I lived at T Wharf in Boston to engage Hauk in conversation on rare occasions.

However, the person who told me more about stone sloops than anyone else was my cousin, Miss Adelaide Erskine Snow of Rockland, Maine. I had heard stories about Cousin Addie long before we met, including the tale of how her adventuresome spirit once frightened her father when he looked up to see her high in the air walking along a spar on a square-rigger tied up at a Rockland wharf.

Addie told me that the stone sloops and schooners—for many were built as sloops and changed into schooners—were necessarily broad of beam and full-bellied craft which carried three items—stone, rock, and granite blocks.

It is interesting that such a large proportion of the stone sloops should hail from the relatively small island of Chebeague. Chebeague sloops and their men were known up and down the Atlantic coast. At first they proclaimed on their stern the fact that they hailed from the town of Cumberland, in which Chebeague is located, but around the 1870's the government ruled that Portland, Maine, their port of entry, should be identified on the stern of all the stone sloops of the area.

Stone slooping as such began in 1795, and within fifty years almost every harbor in Massachusetts was receiving material delivered by the stone sloops.

At Crotch Island in Penobscot Bay, tens of thousands of tons of granite stone were quarried. In most cases it was shipped by Chebeague stone sloops to all parts of the country.*

My cousin Addie told me that for carrying stone the craft were unbeatable, but that reefing them in a storm was not easy. When she was two years old Addie had a stone sloop or schooner named for her. In 1898, at the height of the Portland Gale off the shores of Cape Cod, that craft is believed to have collided with the steamer *Portland* to send the 291-foot sidewheeler to the bottom. Addie treasured the medicine-chest cover marked *ADDIE E. SNOW* which washed ashore among the wreckage after the disaster.

*Quarrying at Crotch Island began in 1871, but by 1945 the handwriting on the wall could be seen. By 1968 the quarries were only memories, as glass, cement, and steel brought granite quarrying practically to an end.

Addie also mentioned the loss of a stone sloop off Graves Light in Boston Harbor during the middle part of the nineteenth century. Captain John Ross and his two sons, John and Walter, froze to death in the rigging of their craft. The exact date of the tragedy is not known.

Columns brought to Boston by the stone sloops were used in building the 1895 addition to the Boston State House, while the 555-foot-high Washington Monument was "backed up" with granite from Rockland, Maine, brought by stone sloops to New York, from where freight trains completed the journey.

The granite for Halfway Rock Light was freighted there by the Chebeague sloop *Yankee* in 1869. Almost every fort and lighthouse along the Atlantic coast has received rock or stones by way of the stone sloops.

4

Sebascodegan Island

Government Chart 315 shows that famed Sebascodegan Island lies eastward of Harpswell Neck and has approximately 5791 acres of land. The name Sebascodegan was derived from an Indian word, the exact meaning of which has been lost in the mist of many generations. Some authorities explain the name as meaning that the area was a good place for hunting, whereas others suggest that the word means "more than satisfactory measure." Still another interpretation is that it stands for the Indian term for marshy ground, or *sebas-low*.

Shortly before the year 1640 Francis Small and his wife arrived on the island, and their baby was the first white child born at Sebascodegan. A Nicholas Shapleigh is said to have purchased the Sebascodegan property from a sagamore, paying a satisfactory amount of tobacco, three guns, and an unspecified amount of wampum in return.

Later Harvard College inherited the island, but by 1733 William Condy was able to lease the entire area for twenty geese!

Herbert Jones states that the early schoolteachers on Sebascodegan made quite an impression with their "three-cornered hats, long single-breasted coats with broad tails, and buckle shoes." They carried ivory-headed canes, which they were not afraid to use on pupils who deserved a few gentle whacks.

What is believed to be the first boardinghouse for sailors in the Casco Bay region was opened at Sebascodegan in the year 1672 by a Tory proprietor named Eastman. Located on the eastern side of Cundy's Point, the building was lavishly painted green and bore the name Green House. The "house" had quite a reputation, and no one in the vicinity claimed that "gentle virtue" was always practiced there. What it lacked in orderly conduct, however, it made up in patriotism.

During the Revolution many plots against the British were secretly hatched at Green House, in spite of the Tory landlord, and one plan in particular ended in a minor American naval victory that the English sea captains never forgot.

Up to the time of the incident it had become the custom for British privateers to sail in and around the Casco Bay Islands at will, and during the early months of the Revolution several American coasters actually fell prey to their raids. Captain Linnacum of the armed British schooner *Picaroon* was among the British captains adept at this practice.

When the final plans of the plot to put an end to one raider were discussed, the men agreed that the Patriots would meet aboard a fourteen-ton schooner rather than at Green House. Thirty of the men under the command of Colonel Purrington met on the schooner the following morning.

The vessel sailed out to a location near Seguin Island to lie in wait for the *Picaroon*, which soon came sailing along anxious for another capture. Suddenly the American craft jibed and came up on the British warship's quarter. A single shot killed the man at the wheel of the *Picaroon* shortly after he had been boasting that he would never "dodge at the flash of a Yankee gun." The volleys of the men of Sebascodegan sent all the Britishers who could still walk down below on the *Picaroon*, and they soon cried for "quarter."

The remains of the unfortunate helmsman, whose name was Shepard, were taken ashore on Sebascodegan and buried at Shepard's Point, as it is known today.

Gurnet Bridge connects Sebascodegan Island with the mainland near Buttermilk Point. Crossing over to the island, a visitor realizes the truth of Herbert Jones' statement made to me in 1946 that if you are a victim of "an age which idolizes speed . . . you will miss much of Maine's essential loveliness." Jones went on to say that one should travel slowly if he wishes to enjoy the full flavor of its scenery. Henry Beston emphasized the same thought when I met him three years later in Damariscotta, Maine, during my 1,158-mile hike from Canada. He stated that "in an auto everything is a travel movie in which the windshield becomes the screen. There is no sense of reality," concluded the author of *Outermost House.*

The residents of Harpswell and its many islands, which include Sebascodegan, Orr's, Bailey, Pond, Haskell, Malaga, Ragged, Bombazeen, Flag, Mark, Eastern Mark, Turnip, and Uncle Zeke, rightly believe that the region is about as perfect as one can ever find. There is a sense of tranquility throughout the area. When Robert Tristram Coffin wrote his autobiographical novel, *Lost Paradise,* it was centered around the Harpswell peninsula and the islands that surround it. Incidentally, many of my ancestors and collateral ancestors are buried in the cemeteries there. Elder Elisha Snow was born at Brunswick on March 20, 1739, and moved to Harpswell shortly afterward with his father Deacon Isaac Snow.*

According to Chart 315, Harpswell Neck is about eight miles in length, and many of its various islands parallel the mainland. If one does not pay attention in the manner of Jones or Beston, he might easily cross the bridge from Sebascodegan without

*I have the beautiful desk of Elisha's son Larkin, who was born in Harpswell in 1778.

realizing it to find himself on Casco Bay's Orr's Island.

Many residents of Sebascodegan still cling to the theory that when Martin Pring, who set sail from Wales in the year 1603, landed and set up a "small barricado to keepe diligent watch and ward," it was in Casco Bay at Sebascodegan. Actually the location was in what is now the vicinity of Plymouth, Massachusetts. Pring gave Plymouth Bay the name Whitson Bay, and wrote his estimate of the latitude as "41 degrees and odde minutes," not the latitude of Sebascodegan, which is much closer to 43 degrees and 30 minutes.

Without question, Martin Pring did establish a trading post in New England to deal with the Indians, at which time, he notes, "we used them kindly and gave them divers sorts of our meanest Merchandise." The Indians around Plymouth were fascinated by the playing on a zither by "a youth in our company . . . in whose homely Music they took great delight."

Do not misunderstand me. Pring, of course, visited Sebascodegan Island before he went south, and the heritage of his stay on the island should always be acknowledged.

In the year 1720, long after Pring left Sebascodegan Island, Samuel Boone arrived there from Rhode Island and purchased half of the entire island, along with half of Harpswell Neck and half of Chebeague.

Thirteen years later, assisted by the Royal prerogative, the Pejepscot Proprietors moved in to establish their ownership of the immediate area including Boone's property. Sebascodegan was then leased to William Cady and William Condy and their associates, but the fishing and mineral rights were not included. Cundy's Harbor is named for William Condy, although the spelling is not exactly the same. Four years later a visitor could count twenty families on the island, but then the fearsome Indians came and drove many of them away.

The legend of Judith Howard, a colonial resident of unusual abilities, according to Margaret Burr Todd, is partly true and partly apocryphal. As it has come down through the years, it seems that Judith was one of those ladies possessed not only of rugged individuality but of outstanding independence as well. While not knowing about green thumbs and the like, Judith had the ability to take roots and herbs and change them into health-giving salves and brews.

Just where truth and legend join cannot be discovered today, but without question the inhabitants of Sebascodegan Island still tell stories of her miraculous cures, particularly in the field of bad burns and painful ulcers. In addition, she was known to be able to reduce a fever in aching bodies and take the misery from tired bones.

Her jealous neighbors, remembering the Salem witch trials, wondered if Judith was not really a witch herself, who received her inspiration from Mephistopheles. They did not take any action against her during her life, but when she died they remembered that she had cautioned them against burying her anywhere near an Indian medicine squaw* who was interred at Cundy's Harbor. Naturally they buried her near the squaw's grave to spite her.

It was not long before manifestations began, indicating that the neighbors had made a great mistake. The very night of Judith's funeral noises were heard all over the village, and on the following night more sounds of troubled souls were heard. Finally, after a week of nightly sounds and weird voices, the women of Sebascodegan decided definitely that they had been wrong in ignoring Judith's admonition.

Warming their "cold courage with rum," they took a yoke of oxen to her grave at Cundy's Harbor, and dug down into the earth to pull up her casket. Artist Draper Hill is at his best in his sketch of the women of Sebascodegan lifting the coffin high

*The squaw, Old Lambo, who was reputed to visit an undersea cave at times and to have done wonders with rattlesnake venom, was active during King Philip's War, according to legend.

in the air as the local preacher gives his blessing to the gathering.

The coffin was transported to another part of the island where it still reposes to this day, far from the influence of Old Lambo.

5

Bailey Island

After enjoying excellent sea food at the island restaurant, one is ready for the exploration of Bailey Island, both past and present. The island was named for Deacon Timothy Bailey, who married his second wife, Hannah Curtis, in the year 1743 at Hanover, Massachusetts. He eventually settled on the island that now bears his name.

Apparently Hannah purchased the island from the North Yarmouth Proprietors for the "price of a pound of tobacco and a gallon of rum," dispossessing Will Black, who had lived on the island with his parents for many years and believed his title was a legal one. Black moved his family across the stretch of water called Will's Gut to nearby Orr's Island.

Historians tell us that in the confines of Mackerel Cove, Deacon Bailey built a log cabin relatively close to a spring of cool water. It is said that the Indians had told him that the Great Spirit had presented the spring to the red men. After his long career hunting and fishing elsewhere in Maine, Indian chieftain Mingo, as he grew older, returned to Bailey Island. He wished to be buried in the area near the spring so that his spirit would always remain in the vicinity that meant so much to his Indian ancestors.

The Baileys promised Mingo that they would not reveal the location where they buried him, and they kept their word. Mingo's grave has never been found. Mingo's Cave today recalls the famed chieftain to those of the present generation.

During the migration of Massachusetts families away from the outskirts of Boston, Bailey Island beckoned to men who were anxious to improve their position in life. The usual settler became a fisherman and a farmer, and in this way found a year-round occupation.

Then there were those who cut and shipped wood to other ports such as Boston, Salem, and even New York.

Deacon Bailey did not allow the members of the community to neglect their spiritual welfare, from time to time engaging visiting ministers and preachers to satisfy the needs of the island. Herbert Jones is the authority for the story of the enthusiastic parson who told Bailey, "Your island is like the origin of your name—Ballium, a rampart. Truly it is like a sheet anchor. It will hold up like God's truth." The preacher spoke in a small frame building on the island.

Although spiritual warmth was present, for many years there was no school on the island. It is said that Deacon Timothy Bailey decided finally that the youngsters were in need of education, and after gathering enough money from his flock, he hired Daniel Sullivan as a teacher. Sullivan was a good instructor, but on occasion school could not be in session because of Sullivan's habit of overindulgence in the demon rum. When the time came for a spree, Sullivan would close school for a relatively extended vacation of a week or more. One particular period arrived when the absence of the teacher led to a vote by the inhabitants that the teaching expenses should be forgotten, and that funds raised for education should be diverted to paying the honest expenses of the Bailey Island selectmen. Sullivan returned before this plan could be carried out.

The demon rum, however, was considered necessary during house-raising festivities. When house- or barn-raising get-togethers were held, every able-bodied man on Bailey Island presented himself at the chosen site for the new building. Then, with a will, the jovial workers lifted the massive timbers from the horizontal position on the ground and soon supported and braced them to form the framework of the house.

After the job was completed, the mugs and pitchers full of rum were passed around. It is said that once in a while too-frequent indulgence produced many an unsteady hand.

One of the earliest buildings still standing on Bailey Island is the Gardiner House, said to have been erected in the year 1818. Located some distance away from the road, it is near a deep well. Thomas Merryman, who distinguished himself by marrying Deacon Bailey's daughter, built the house using the remains of the Bailey log cabin. Merryman journeyed to Pond Island to get mussel shells, which he crushed to make lime needed for plastering the walls.

The house of Captain Roduck Johnson, sketched by Herbert Jones in 1946, was built high up on a Bailey Island hill in 1763. The story is that about this time Captain Johnson, otherwise known as Jot, was sailing to the West Indies. One day his craft touched at Anguilla on St. Martin's Island, and there he fell in love with a girl of French-Dutch parentage. Returning to Bailey Island, he began the construction of his home, which soon became known as Jot's House. When he had finished his task, he returned to Anguilla to propose to his sweetheart and was accepted.

Soon the two were married and he brought her back to Bailey Island with him. At the time his was the only residence in the immediate area, and although there was an outstanding vista of the ocean, the view in winter was said to be rather bleak and lonely.

Nevertheless, although she pined for her St. Martin's home, she was soon busy anticipating the arrival of their firstborn. Within a few years they had produced a large family and she was content at Jot's House.

Another resident of Bailey Island began life in Ireland. As a youth of twenty-one, Michael Sinnett was shanghaied at Dublin, the victim of the captain of an American ship. Lured aboard the craft, he and a friend were carried off to Boston as members of the crew. On their arrival in Boston, Sinnett was sold as an indentured servant and became a farmer for Joseph Orr at Orr's Island to pay for his passage money. Just why passage money was needed when he had been lured aboard the craft has not come down to us, but in any case he moved to Bailey Island after he had paid off his supposed indebtedness. Later he fell in love and married a girl in the Orr family, a Mary Ward of Hingham, Massachusetts.

His troubles were not over. Starting a farm on the mainland, Sinnett had the additional misfortune to be captured by a press-gang while he was alone on the farm. This time he was taken to New York. He served in the siege of Quebec and was discharged in 1763 at the declaration of peace.

The story goes that he then made his way back to where his wife was living at Orr's Island, arriving while she was milking cows in the barn. According to the story, which may be apocryphal, he walked up behind her and merely placed his hand on her shoulder to announce his return. After a joyful reunion, he settled down to farming and later purchased thirty acres of land on Bailey Island, where he lived in happiness for the rest of his life.

During the War of 1812 a fort was built at the end of Bailey Island. An enemy vessel appeared in Mackerel Cove, and as the men were on the mainland, the women dressed in men's clothes and took positions around the cove. When the British marines landed, two old men told the Englishmen who had come ashore from the warship that the woods ashore were filled with American troops and that they would be wise to go back to their battleship. The ruse worked, and the British marines sailed away.*

The Sinnett family continued to experience unusual adventures. Two Sinnett boys were lured from their fishing smack by the British warship *Rattler*, and were kept for a week while the British used their craft to reconnoiter and explore the enemy's coastline. The boys were released a week later, and their fishing smack was returned to them.

On another occasion a British barge began to chase a Bailey Island coaster owned by David Johnson, and as the two craft drew closer to shore, Captain James Sinnett noticed them. In charge of the single cannon guarding Mackerel Cove, Sinnett sent out a messenger in a dory to shout across to the British commander that he would give the Britishers "a reasonable time to leave," and then he would open fire with the cannon. The barge withdrew.

As it did in many other communities, the War of 1812 was followed by hard times on Bailey Island. By 1836 there were only ten houses on the island, all occupied by fishermen, for the other families had moved ashore.

As the years have gone by romantic names have been attached to various locations on Bailey Island, the Giant's Steps being the most famous. Also known as the Devil's Stairway, it can be called a perfect flight of large stone steps evenly cut by nature into the sea wall. At high tide a modestly sized craft is able to come in to get passengers aboard here. Roughly forty inches high each, the stairs with their even measurements have made many believe that man had something to do with their

---

*A similar ruse also worked during the War of 1812 at Scituate, Massachusetts. Rebecca and Abigail Bates, one playing the fife and the other beating a drum, made the British redcoats think an American army was awaiting them, and the marines returned to their warship off Scituate. The girls have been called the "American Army of Two."

formation. One legendary tale is that pirates used the Giant's Steps to land and bury treasure around the island.

Other places of interest I have visited on the island include the Thunder Hole, Profile Rock, and Pinnacle Rock. Jaquith Gut and Water Cove should also interest the visitor.

A true treasure tale I wrote in 1951* has John Wilson as the hero. Out hunting for ducks in the vicinity of the Cedar Ledges, which are a little to the southwest of Two Bush Island, he slipped on the kelp and rockweed, fetching up in a deep hole. There at the bottom of the cavity was a copper kettle filled with golden doubloons. Telling no one when he reached home, he left the island in a short time carrying a large, heavy suitcase and headed for Boston. In that year of 1840 he was able to sell his gold for about $12,000, a tidy sum 135 years ago. Wilson lived prosperously for the remainder of his life, and not until his death did the treasure find become known. At that time papers dealing with his visit to Boston became available to the members of his family.

The tale of Captain Wardwell, another resident of Bailey Island, is of interest. One day this master mariner was particularly anxious to have an outstandingly successful voyage. Because he was superstitious, Wardwell gave a well-known medium of the area, a Mrs. Leach, a bushel of wheat to ensure his having a successful trip. It is said that his sea journey well repaid him for his donation of wheat to the Harpswell clairvoyant.

Almost every area has stories about a headless ghost. There are tales told of one down at Deer Island in Boston Harbor, and still another ghost without a head haunts an area off Cape Breton Island. The people of Bailey Island often tell incredulous visitors about the headless pirate who appeared during one Christmas season and the two months following. Several of the

* *True Tales of Buried Treasure*, page 178.

details, however, should bear careful scrutiny. The headless pirate was often seen straddling a "milk-white horse with wings," and was usually observed on moonless nights "flying up and down the road about twenty feet in the air."

The male members of the Sinnett clan dominated the fishing out of Bailey Island for generations, but during the last years of the nineteenth century fishing out of Casco Bay in the old fashion began to be replaced by tuna fishing craft, which have established great records, and are attracting attention all over the United States. Incidentally, back in 1877 a tuna fish, then called horse mackerel, was weighed in at 1,100 pounds. The weighing took place at Lowell's Cove, Orr's Island. According to historians Margaret Burr Todd and Charles Todd in their delightful booklet *Beautiful Harpswell*, Emore Gilliam harpooned the tuna, which gave Emore "a wild, fast ride" before giving up.

6

Steamers Around Casco Bay

In the pages of the Portland *Argus* can be found the following notice from August 13, 1822. As far as I can tell from extensive research, the notice is probably the first ever placed anywhere in Maine involving a steamboat:

STEAMBOAT KENNEBEC WILL LEAVE UNION WHARF PORTLAND AT FOUR O'CLOCK FOR NORTH YARMOUTH TO SPEND THE DAY. WILL RETURN ON THURSDAY TO TAKE PASSENGERS TO THE ISLAND AS USUAL. IF REQUIRED WILL STOP AT WEEK'S WHARF TO RECEIVE AND LAND PASSENGERS. FOR TICKETS APPLY TO MR. A. W. TINK-HAM'S STORE.

Steamboat historian Francis B. C. Bradlee tells us that a local poet, bank messenger, and constable named Lewis Pease recorded the event with a slur toward sailing vessels:

> A fig for all your clumsy craft
> Your pleasure boats and packets,

The *Steamboat* lands you safe and soon
At Mansfield's, Trott's, or Brackett's.

Although the poem boasted of the superiority of steam over sail, actually this was not true. The *Kennebec* was far from first class, for not only did she possess an engine so weak that she hardly had power to steam against the tide in Casco Bay, but when she had been put together in Bath the builders used the hull of an old flat-bottomed scow which Captain Seward Porter had purchased for "excursions in shoal water."

In spite of the poet's quatrain, real deepwater sailors were quick to snort at the *Kennebec*, and before long labeled her the "ground hog." She was often in trouble. It seems hard to be-

lieve but there are stories of passengers being called upon to assist in turning the paddlewheels, not quite in the manner of squirrels inside a circular cage, but by putting their weight on the individual paddles as they came by.

The earliest steamers running regularly to the islands in Casco Bay from Portland were the *Express* and the *Gazelle*, owned and operated by the Peak's Island Steamboat Company, later known as the Forest City Steamboat Company. The *Gazelle* was subsequently lengthened and renamed the *Forest City*.

The business was relatively prosperous, attracting a competing group of mariners and landlubbers who decided to start an opposition line called the Union Steamboat Company. Their first craft was the *Emita*, which was soon followed by the *Cadet*. In a short time the Union group became the Star Line Steamboat Company.

It was seen that the two lines might do better if they could get together as one large organization, and Captain B. J. Willard of Portland, then the general manager of the Forest City Company, effected a consolidation of the two lines under the name Casco Bay Steamboat Company.

C. W. T. Goding was elected general manager of the firm. In July, 1887, a new steamer was put into service, the propeller craft *Forest Queen*. Large and safe, she ran all the year long.

For some years after the turn of the century the *Forest Queen* continued to run efficiently, having been joined by two additional screw-propeller craft, the *Pilgrim* and the *Merriconeag*.

I have made a list of craft that have served the Casco Bay region down through the years. For easy reading they are arranged in alphabetical fashion. Of course, this list cannot be considered all-inclusive, for only a life study could possibly mention every craft of importance that has negotiated the delightful waters between the mainland and the many islands.

Abenaki	*Forest City*	*Merriconeag*
Alice	*Forest Queen*	*Mineola*
Antelope	*Gazelle*	*Minnehaha*
Aucocisco I	*Greenwood*	*Nellie G. I*
Aucocisco II	*Gorden*	*Nellie G. II*
Berkeley	*Gurnet*	*Nellie G. III*
Cadet	*Haidee*	*Pejepscot*
Casco	*Henrietta*	*Phantom*
Charles A. Warren	*Isis*	*Pilgrim*
Chebeague	*Island Adventure*	*Sabino*
Corinna	*Island Belle*	*Sebascodegan*
Cornelia H.	*Island Holiday*	*Spring*
El Dorado	*Island Romance*	*Sunshine*
Emita I	*Kennebec*	*Swampscott*
Emita II	*Machigonne*	*Tourist*
Enterprise	*Madeleine*	*Tourist II*
Express	*Maquoit*	*Venture*
	Mary G. Libby	

7

Great Diamond Island

Great Diamond Island, between Little Diamond and Cow Island, is across the channel from Peak's Island in Casco Bay. Robert Laughlin, who wrote about it very effectively in 1972, notes that it has passed through many vicissitudes.

When Mrs. Snow and I landed there in 1958, we pulled our canoe high above the tide and found ourselves near a small cavelike opening in the rocks. For the next two hours we explored the island, visiting many of the fortifications and underground passageways. We eventually learned that the island has seven coves and three points of land. As author Laughlin tells us, the coves are Peabody, Seal, Indian, Pleasant, Diamond, Elm, and Gilson, while the three points of land are fairly close together in the general area of the pier and are Sand Bar, Rock, and Echo. I don't know how many of these locations my brother Donald visited when he did his soldiering at Fort McKinley here more than a generation ago, but knowing his ability in long-distance swimming, I presume he visited them all, or at least saw them from the water.

Between the years 1628 and 1658 Great Diamond Island

went through a period of long, confused ownership, as there were conflicting claims for possession under several patents and grants.

The most important reference to the island occurs in a lease for two thousand years, given in 1635 by Sir Ferdinando Gorges, proprietor of all the land between the Piscataqua River and the Kennebec. Gorges granted to George Cleeves and Richard Tucker "one island adjacent to the said premises and now in the tenor of the occupation of the said George Cleeves and Richard Tucker commonly called or known by the name of Hogg Island," which is Diamond Island today.

Cleeves sold Hogg Island in 1658 to Thomas Kimball, a merchant of Charlestown, who in 1663 relinquished it for twenty-five pounds to Edward Tyng of Boston. It then passed through the hands of several proprietors until in 1743 Ephraim Jones and James Gooding sold their interest in it to Deacon James Milk. He came into complete possession in 1756. In 1762 Deacon Milk, who lived in Falmouth on Exchange Street near Milk Street, married his second wife, the widow Deering of Kittery. Deacon Milk with his five children and the widow Deering with her eleven combined to make a large family at their Diamond Island home. When the deacon died, their many children inherited the property, which was divided among them. Eventually Nathaniel Deering acquired the rights to the island, which, at his death, he left to his two children, James and Mary.

His daughter Mary married Commodore Edward Preble, and the Preble family retained possession of the island for more than a century.

Incidentally, there are several writers on Casco Bay who speak of a Governor Belehen who held a conference at Great Diamond Island with two hundred Indians in the year 1732. Actually there never was a Governor Belehen, but there was a Governor Jonathan Belcher of the province of Massachusetts

Bay, of which Maine was a part, duly appointed by the rules of the Second Charter. Governor Belcher was the area's leader from August 10, 1730, until August 14, 1741, when Governor William Shirley took the reigns of office.

Maine's famous artist Charles Codman painted scenes around Diamond Cove in 1829. During this period there were picnics and moonlight sails in the summer and ice boating and even sleighing in the winter to Hogg Island, as Great Diamond was then called. The island was considered the beauty spot of Casco Bay.

Toward the middle of the century Great Hogg Island became a place for fishermen to obtain shelter, water, and possibly timber to make repairs on their vessels.

During the next generation a group of reliable, influential residents gathered together to form an association on the island. Mr. Edward Elwell gives the following account of the initial organization of the Diamond Island Association. On behalf of the residents, on "August 27, 1882, Mr. E. G. P. Smith took refusal of ninety-seven and one-half acres of land on the island, of Messrs. Francis and J. D. Fessenden," on the condition that the sum of $7,679.55 would be raised in thirty-six hours, and this was somehow accomplished.

In his annual report in September, 1883, President E. G. P. Smith reported progress in laying out avenues, streets, parks, and cottage lots at an expense of $700; of cutting away dead spruce and selling it for $2.50 a cord with a profit of $2,400; cutting $1,000 worth of timber for buoys, piling, cribwork, and wharf stringers, with 25,000 board feet sawed into wharf planking. Casco Wharf had been constructed with 100 feet of earth fill and 432 feet of woodwork.

Diamond Cove was so called on charts long before the island name was changed from Great Hogg to Great Diamond. In the cove the veins of quartz and pockets of crystals were seen to sparkle when the sun struck them, which led to its name.

A story has been told that a rather rotund lady, before the name Diamond was adopted, stated that when mail should start to come to the island, she would not relish the idea of having it sent to her with Great Hogg as her address. The change from Hogg to Diamond Island was, of course, a gradual one.

In 1886 the firm of Ilsley and Cummings made a survey that showed 506 cottage lots covering 126 acres, 30 avenues and streets requiring 37 acres, and 76 cottage lots that remained in the Association. The steamboat accommodations were good. The Forest City boats landed on the south side and the steamer *Isis* on the west and east.

In 1889 the total number of cottages was 57 and the population, exclusive of the farm, was 300. The Portland Club erected a summer clubhouse on the high knoll now owned by Bruce Laughlin.

The Association continually made improvements on the island. Kerosene street lights discarded by the city of Portland were supplied to the island. In the basement of the island's restaurant Mr. Shaw operated a grocery store. The water company arranged a contract to build an iron standpipe of 140,000-gallon capacity and to construct a reservoir near the Moody Spring fifty by twelve feet in size.

In 1892 the firm of Morrill and Ross ran the restaurant and the grocery store, paying $125 rent to the Association. The Portland City Government was requested to appoint Mr. Benjamin Gribben as a policeman for the summer. On July 4 of the same year Elwell Hall was dedicated, the original restaurant having been remodeled in accordance with plans by John Calvin Stevens.

The channel to Casco Wharf needed dredging in 1895, and because the *Isis* was frequently disabled, patronage had gone to the other line. The Falmouth Foreside Steamboat Company agreed to do the dredging and to provide service.

Farms in the generations before the present century were

vital factors in the daily life of insular communities, even more than on the mainland. Today their value on an island has been diminished by our changing economy. Through the years the farm at Great Diamond Island has been very active. Isaac Thurlow ran the Deering farm and was succeeded first by J. S. Irish and, in 1896, by Mr. Holland and Mr. Merrill. They provided the residents with meat, eggs, vegetables, and ice. The farm later created problems when the buildings needed repair and prices for produce were considered too high. Hay cut on individual lots often caused complaints and controversy.

The year 1898 was the start of the first discordant era on the island. Cottages were largely vacant because of the war with Spain and the fact that the fortifications being built were destroying the scenic beauty of the eastern end of the island.

In the early 1900's an acetylene gas plant was in operation on the island, so that several cottages were equipped with gas and the streets were lighted by gas lamps.

In 1914 Casco Wharf was carried away by ice. It was repaired in November, but a storm a few days later carried away 150 feet of the wharf again. Repairs were not made until the spring. Sixteen cottages were broken into during the winter, and even a sizable rowboat disappeared from under a cottage far from the shore.

It must be remembered that important changes occurred in the way of life during this period. Automobiles had come in, and the more prosperous residents could now give up their island retreats and travel by car to enlarge their horizons. No doubt many of the youth had come to think, "There's nothing to do around here. Why can't I go where the action is?"

Many patriotic cottage owners leased their properties to the overflow of personnel at Fort McKinley for year-round habitation. As a result of winter use, some cottages designed only for summer were nearly ruined.

During the first two decades after the formation of the Association, people of affluence owned the cottages. They enjoyed the use of an excellent nine-hole golf course, two tennis courts, mooring and docking facilities for their boats on both sides of the island, and a private means of water transportation to and from the city by their own steamboat, the *Isis*. The *Isis* ran from Portland to both the west side Casco Landing and the landing in Diamond Cove. We are told that although the distance to their cottages may have been greater, many coming back from work on a pleasant summer evening delighted in the longer boat ride and the walk through the woods from Diamond Cove.

It was apparent that a good number of original islanders were nature lovers, as indicated by the development of various roads and paths through the woods and to the cliffs, where an outstanding picnic area was laid out. The rustic benches, steps, and handrails over some of the ledges, and the maintenance of the ice ponds, were a nature lover's delight. Several of the roads and paths through the woods were passable by bicycle.

The decision of the U.S. government to build Fort McKinley on the northeastern half of the island had a tremendous effect upon the financial and cultural concepts of the Association members. Many did not wish to see their sanctuary disrupted, while others saw an opportunity for financial gain. The land was finally taken by right of eminent domain and the government paid $149,850 in damages. Great Diamond has never regained its original character since the fort became part of the island.

It was clear that with the arrival of the military, the island would change in character. The peaceful summer island community that had purchased one half of Great Diamond Island and controlled the rest, now lost approximately half of its area to the military. From a total population of about 350 during the summer, now there would be a year-round military population of 1,000.

The building of massive gun emplacements, barracks, homes

for officers, warehouses for supplies and munitions, stables for army mules, and magazines for mines and explosives was disturbing enough without the firing of three-, six-, and eight-inch guns, as well as twelve-inch mortars and submarine mines out in Hussey Sound.

The situation was somewhat less disturbing to the younger generation. The change afforded male companionship for the island's young ladies and a sense of adventure for the men and boys as they became familiar with the various companies, and the locations and operations of the different batteries. There was Ramsay with two three-inch rifles, Carpenter with six-inch cannon, Honeycutt with two eight-inch disappearing rifles, Berry with twelve-inch cannon, and many others that were later put in.

One outstanding thrill for everyone was the ability to pick up the sight of a mortar projectile about one quarter up in its trajectory and follow it to the top of its course and down again to the point of disappearance just before it splashed into the sea near the target that was being towed by one of the army vessels. Four craft were engaged for the towing, the *Henry Wilson*, *General Randall*, *General Bachelder*, and *Drew*. An exciting incident occurred when inexperienced plotters made an error and a shot went through the stack of the *Drew*.

Thunderstorms seemed bigger and better in the early years of the century. They would come down the Presumpscot River and sweep majestically across the bay to concentrate on Great Diamond, with lightning occasionally hitting a cottage or tree.

Ancient Captain Johnson sold fireworks at Fourth of July time from his sloop *Excaliber*, tied up during this period at the stone wharf. While many considered the old captain a maritime hermit and a person to be avoided, there were those who delighted in sending him cakes and pies to supplement his meager diet. The historian who said that it was thought that the captain had a trained rat that sat at the table and ate with him had an unusual imagination. After Captain Johnson died his sloop was used in a movie and was blown up as part of the plot.

During World War II the Hall was closed, tennis and golf discontinued, and normal island social affairs ceased.

The overwhelming importance of the Association asserted itself in the readjustment period after the war. In 1954 Jack and Ethel White, aided by fifty dollars put up as an investment by each of seventeen residents, began operation of the store. In this year also a work crew of members rebuilt the tennis court.

In 1958 a notation appears in the records: "The chairman of the budget committee explained by graft the probable income and expenses for the ensuing year." The inference was not intended, of course, as the "graft" (graph) was merely a chart!

The year 1961 was memorable. Bids were received for the purchase of Fort McKinley. The Great Diamond Association had a representative at the bidding, but he had no authority to bid. Mr. Montalbano purchased the 191-acre property that year for $42,350.

At this time the Casco Bay Lines wharves were condemned and island commuters had to travel by lobster boats and other craft to and from the city until the Maine Port Authority rebuilt the wharves.

When King Resources came into the bay in 1970 and took over the former Navy Oil Depot on Long Island, the property was sold to them for a reported quarter of a million dollars. However, by 1972, Fort McKinley, owned by King Resources, was in the hands of receivers.

8

Little Diamond Island

Jessie Stuart, in her outstanding *Short History of Diamond Island*, tells us of the "ups and downs" of this delightful summer colony which flourished in Casco Bay between the years 1910 and 1965, and still carries on in 1975 with hopes for the future. No matter what is happening elsewhere in the world, there is a great fellowship at Little Diamond.

Stuart, a retired Simmons College professor, writes that from 1900 until 1910 the island changed from a working farm and grazing land to a summer colony. There were about twenty-five cottages on the south side of the island, while the northern half was owned in part by the diocese of Portland of the Roman Catholic Church and used as a vacation camp for the girls from St. Elizabeth's Orphanage in the city.

Summer colonies were most popular all over Maine just before World War I. Boston and New York at that time were connected to Maine by boat, and people from all over the country were learning about the "beauties and charms" of the Maine coast.

In this period one cottage on Little Diamond was visited by

both out-of-town residents and islanders—the present Milliken
building on the top of the hill. It was then run by the Nissen
family, the members of which became known as bakers all over
New England. Unbelievably, the cost for an adult for three
meals a day was four dollars a week! Boarders, when there was
room for them, paid extra for overnight accommodations.

In 1908 George W. Brown began carrying out ambitious
plans for promoting Little Diamond Island as a summer
colony. Buying forty lots under the title of the Maine Coast
Realty Company, he put in a new water system, planned roads
and streets, introduced sun-heated salt-water baths, and provided a public restaurant. Unfortunately, although the project
showed promise at first, it did not succeed. When everything
collapsed, members of the Little Diamond Association took
over what they could on November 13, 1912.

General Frederick Keating, British vice-consul at Portland,
bought the restaurant and the other facilities. He did very well
for several years, but at the end of World War I he left Portland.
At that time Keating's original Casino and bathhouse were
sold to the Association. Ralph Bryant subsequently bought the
Casino and moved it to the southwestern tip of the island. The
Keating cottage was opened as the new Casino in 1924.

Two years later electricity came to Little Diamond, and the
change was not popular with "old Charlie," who had been the
lamplighter on the island so long he considered it his lifetime
position. In his nightly routine of lighting the gas lamps he was
accompanied by his little pet pig. Charlie finally realized, however, that electricity was on the island to stay, and as Jessie
Stuart tells us, "Charlie and his pig disappeared from Little
Diamond forever."

By the coming of World War II the fortunes of Little Diamond Island showed a definite decline, and although wartime
activities in Casco Bay were many, the island did not share the
wartime prosperity.

One of the real personalities on the island was Elmer Bachelder, who came to Little Diamond in 1911. He claimed that Venice at sunset could not possibly equal the beauties of Little Diamond Island, and in this he was seconded by Captain William Hill, who until his death at eighty-five in 1945 was an outstanding leader of the community.

Although between World War II and 1975 an entirely new generation moved to Little Diamond Island, the names of Stowell, Cushman, Smith, Ward, James, and Chamberlain are remembered whenever the residents gather for the weekend suppers.

Mrs. Elizabeth Hobbs and her husband Frank of South Portland are strong personalities at the island today. She told me of how Danny Carr would bring across groceries and other necessities in the truck at low tide from Great Diamond Island, and she so regretted the day when this service ended. Residents now take their wheelbarrows and other vehicles to the Casco Bay wharf to bring home their supplies.

Mrs. Hobbs praised the Casino for its ability to serve a dual purpose, with upstairs record hops for the younger generation matched by delightful weekend suppers downstairs at frequent intervals.

Mrs. Hobbs recalled the career of George Brown. Although he eventually failed in his plans for the island, he was able to erect the original Casino, whose name is perpetuated in the present building. She told me that Ted Rand, who took over the coast guard buoy station, is able and willing to supply vital necessities as he runs the outstandingly efficient marina at the Little Diamond wharf.

Social life down through the years has been highlighted by a club formed by the women of the island. First called the Macao Club, when the ladies later decided to enlarge the organization it was given the name Macao-Cogawesco Club, and finally the Macao was dropped from the title. Cogawesco was an Indian chief said to have been a resident of Little Diamond Island during the seventeenth century. Mrs. George Haynes was responsible for starting the club.

When we visited Little Diamond quite a few years ago by canoe, we paddled across to the ship graveyard, which is just off the island. It was a strange feeling to go aboard these rotting hulks on which generations ago so many happy islanders and visitors enjoyed the pleasant tours around Casco Bay.

Another interesting thought we indulged in was that for its size Little Diamond probably has more channel markers and buoys in the water around the island than any similar location in Casco Bay. We counted eight!

I admire the present residents of Little Diamond Island and their determination to succeed. I am sure the future holds much happiness for them.

9

Bustins, Cousins, and Neighboring Islands

In 1960, when George B. Richardson published the history of Bustins Island and Casco Bay, he related how he had been coming to the island since the year 1917. This eighty-four-page book is almost impossible to find these days, but it is so excellent that I will refer to it from time to time.

Bustins Island is located off the Casco Bay mainland across from Flying Point. About the year 1660, according to the early York deeds, John Bustion was identified as owning the island named for him. It is possible that he was an Indian trader at the time. Seven years later he sold the island to William Haines of Pine Point, the location now known as Flying Point.

William Haines attracted attention in 1667 when John Cousins complained about him, calling him a common liar. Haines retaliated by stating that Cousins actually played cards on the Lord's Day! Another islander, John Moshier, son of Hugh Moshier, was indicted for traveling on the Sabbath, but claimed he only moved from his home to the water to save his friend and neighbor, Lane, from drowning. The court evidently did not believe him, and fined John Moshier five shillings and costs, but promised to return the money should Moshier be able to prove the truth of his statement.

In 1700 William Haines' son appears in the records as claiming the lands owned by his father at Pine Point and "Bustions" Island. He stated that his father had improved the lands, and he was one of the children "born in ye said place, North Yarmouth."

George B. Richardson includes in his volume an outstanding 1722 map of Casco Bay, drawn by Boston's Captain Cyprian Southack, whose treasure map of Cape Cod is in my *True Tales of Buried Treasure*. Southack was master of the *Province Galley*, which on several occasions was active in Casco Bay.

On December 15, 1797, James Bibber purchased the rights to Bustins Island from the Jeremiah Powell estate. James Bibber was "a rugged individualist," who employed oxen to dig cellar holes and move rocks and boulders. Bibber died at the age of ninety in 1843, and is buried in the Bibber cemetery on the island, as identified by Charles Guppy, who often ferried summer residents to the mainland. The island for many years was known as Bibber's Island.

Elizabeth Darling Jackson, now of Amherst, New Hampshire, told me in April, 1975, that she had visited almost every part of Bustins Island. She is fond of the island because it is one location where ultramodern facilities have not taken over. "Our home was down near the dock, and there were no street lights in the area," she told me.

Admiral Donald B. MacMillen was at Bustins from time to time. He ran a camp on the island when he was physical director at Worcester Academy around the year 1903, and often sailed across to Bustins in later years.

Three quarters of a century ago the signal calling for the boat to stop at Bustins Island was a large barrel-shaped device on a flagpole. It looked unusual, but it was outstandingly efficient.

In the year 1960 the two old farmhouses were occupied by

the Kitchen family and the Grace family. The Bibber or Swett home was the property of Donald Kitchen, while the Stover or Merrill house was the summer residence of Philip Grace. Both buildings are "interesting studies of old-time home construction."

Author Richardson tells us that Bustins is an island where the summer residents "are to a large extent the same families or their friends who have been coming to the Island for years." It is a way of life for many of them. George B. Richardson concludes with the thought that there is "no place like Bustins."

Writer Bhima Sturtevant suggests that John Cousins, who settled Cousins Island, was probably of the Anglican faith. Born in 1596, he went to school in England. Miss Sturtevant concludes that as he didn't arrive in Boston with the Puritans, Cousins was probably Anglican.

He settled first on the Royal River at Yarmouth with George Felt, who was killed at House Island by Indians.

Cousins bought Cousins Island directly from the great Ferdinando Gorges, and did not lease it as had been done by other settlers.

Cousins appears on several occasions in the records of the period. Often a juror, he also acted as agent for George Cleeves. When he was constable, Cousins appeared before the grand jury in a strange case involving abuse of an Indian, and he was prominent in the slander suit of Mrs. John Winter, who claimed that George Cleeves spoke in a disrespectful manner of her.

Cousins sold half of the island to Richard Bray, who in turn conveyed his property to George Peterson. John probably never married, and as an old man he moved to York. A lady named Mary Hayward, who acted as his housekeeper, inherited his share in Cousins Island when he died at the age of eighty-seven.

Two shipyards were later established at Cousins Island, one at Sandy Point, the other at Birch Point. Yawls, ketches, sloops, and schooners were turned out in effective numbers. A black-smith also set up his shop at the island.

John Cousins would be alarmed at the changes in Cousins Island. Perhaps the greatest are the bridge and the great plant of the Central Maine Power Company at Birch Point on the southern end of the island, where the outline of the high power plant stands against the sky.

I am told that Cousins Island was chosen for the plant because it provides deep and protected anchorage and is close enough to industrial areas; also sea water is practical for cooling the condensers. The power plant was begun in the year 1958 and gains importance in the thoughts of the inhabitants of the area in this period of energy crises.

Writing to me on April 14, 1975, Bess Chaplin tells of her life at Cousins Island. "I was born on Cousins Island, and my father's folks lived and worked there. I have visited the grave-yard where they are all buried.

"My great grandfather, Captain John Hill, was a whaler. He went all around the area in his ships. Cousins was an island where clam digging and fishing was the main thing to do for a living. A flourishing hotel did business there at one time."

Other islands in the general area include Sow and Pigs, Crab, Goose, Gosling, Whaleboat, Pound of Tea, Little Bustins, and Moshier.

Sow and Pigs Islands were owned by Cornelius Soule in 1960. During the Civil War a Chadwick family lived there, and several of the children caught tuberculosis. Catherine Hoyt later lived on the island, and the contraction of her name to Kittoit was well known at the time. Incidentally, when sailing it is wise to pass between the large and small Sow and Pigs Islands only at high tide.

Crab Island is so named because at certain times of tide it is said to resemble a crab with claws extended. However, I have never agreed with this thought, even while passing over it during the Flying Santa run at Christmas. In the 1870's a family built a house on Crab Island, but a fire gutted the building. Another residence was constructed later.

There are two schools of thought concerning the naming of Pound of Tea Island. One group believes the island was so named because it appears to be no larger on a chart than a pound of tea. Equally insistent are those who contend that it was because the island was purchased and paid for with a pound of tea.

Upper and Lower Goose Island and Gosling Islands include several small coves on Lower Goose and a farmhouse erected during the period immediately before the Revolution. Off to the southeast of Lower Goose lie Little French Island and French Island. Shelter Island is to the southeast of Upper Goose. Lower Goose Island was said to have the "fair cows" of all the islands. It is located about a mile east of Bustins Island, which itself is roughly a mile and a half southeast of Wolf Neck on the mainland.

Ledges in the general area include Googins Ledge, Moshier Ledge and Bustins Ledge, around Bustins Island and Old Tom Rock, due north of Cornfield Point on Cousins Island, and Upper Basket Ledge, immediately south of the light at Spruce Point on Cousins Island.

Birch Island, Scrag Island, and White Island are offshore from Merepoint Neck where the Round the World flyers landed in 1924.

Littlejohn's Island, which is connected by bridge to Cousins Island, has a 93-foot high point near the road on its southern point.

Whaleboat Island resembles a whaleboat when seen from the air. Using a little imagination, one may identify on the southeasterly end the "shadow image of two men in a boat."

10

Cushing Island

It had been a battle far more strenuous than I had anticipated. Nevertheless, I had won it. Launching my canoe from Maiden Cove on the Cape Elizabeth mainland, I had reached the bell buoy and the red nun buoy off Catfish Rock, but the wind and tide united to slow the canoe and force me to take extra time, considerably more than I had figured.

In spite of the delay, half an hour after leaving the mainland, I entered Whitehead Passage, although still a substantial distance from a point halfway between Ram Island and Whitehead on Cushing Island. I soon sighted the profile I knew so well, the outline of either a man or a woman high on the rocky cliffs of Cushing Island, a profile whose gender has been debated for more than two centuries.

Although still some distance from shore, I plunged my tandem paddle into the waves with renewed effort and thought of another canoe trip I'd made in the summer of 1954, paddling right across Massachusetts Bay from Race Point Coast Guard Station to Marshfield. That recollection gave me a little extra courage to face the unexpected opposition I was getting.

Soon I was between Trott's Rock and Whitehead itself, where I made several photographs of the profile of what historian Herbert Jones calls the Old Man of Cushing Island. Although I had his book with me, I couldn't quite identify the exact picture he had sketched, and so in an attempt to at least approach Jones' artistry, I recorded with my camera several angle shots of the eons-old Whitehead patriarch or matriarch.

Finally I abandoned my picture taking, tucked the camera away in its waterproof container, and paddled ashore. Resting a short distance from the pier on Cushing Island, I pulled out all my belongings and spread the wet material in the sun to dry.

The chart of Casco Bay shows that Cushing is one of the islands closest to the South Portland mainland off to the westward. House Island is to the northwest, while Peak's Island is directly north, and a little east.

Christopher Levett, the earliest owner of Cushing Island, sold it to a group of English merchants. In turn George Cleeves bought the island. Cleeves had been ordered to leave Richmond's Island, and was then living in what is now Portland. Cleeves gave Cushing Island to his daughter Elizabeth, who married Michael Mitton of Peak's Island. Later their daughter Sarah married James Andrews, with Cushing Island as her dowry!

From 1667 until 1698 Cushing Island was known as Andrews Island, and then it became Portland Island. A fort was built there in 1670 to protect the islanders from the Indians. George Felt reached Cushing Island with a group searching for food, crossed over to House Island, and began to dig clams. The Indians captured the foragers there on House Island, murdering everyone.

To say the least, the history of Cushing Island becomes quite involved, except for those who are genealogical experts. John Rouse of Marshfield, Massachusetts, acquired the island in 1698. That very year, down in the neighboring town of Scituate, Massachusetts, Ezekiel Cushing was born. He later moved to

Provincetown and then to Cape Elizabeth, where he rapidly began to obtain property. Cushing Island, then called Fort Island, was among his acquisitions.

Cushing joined the military forces and became the colonel in command of the county regiment. By this time he was among the more influential men of his day. Elected selectman of the Maine community no less than nine times, he attracted attention as one of the principals in the notorious "Clark Affair" of August, 1755.

Reverend Ephraim Clark had begun preaching in the Purpooduck Parish of what is now Portland, and so great was the effect of his sermons that historians have compared him with the legendary preacher George Whitefield of England.

According to Pastor William Willis, "several people went from this side [of the river] to hear him," indicating that the preacher had more than his share of eighteenth-century charisma. It was then August of 1755.

In the crisis that followed, a grand council of fifteen churches was called. Colonel Cushing, who by this time had had Cushing Island named for him, did not like Clark and wanted to oust him. By a vote of 23 to 18, with two "neuters," Clark was refused installation as pastor. In Reverend Smith's diary, we read that there was a "terrible uproar about Mr. Clark's being poisoned by a Mr. Levitt," but how much truth there was to the allegations and just what happened we shall never know.

Another interesting outcome of the affair was that when twenty-four members of the parish church refused to pay their pledges because of Clark's ouster, they were committed to jail!

In business affairs Cushing was very successful. He ran an amazingly prosperous sailing fleet in the West Indies trade, and at one time his annual profits rivaled those of merchants from both Boston and Salem. The beautiful residence on the mainland in which he lived was a landmark known to almost every resident of the area.

Another man now became interested in Cushing Island. He

was a former inhabitant of Plymouth, Massachusetts, Joshua Bangs. Purchasing the island from Ezekiel Cushing, Bangs soon mortgaged it to his son-in-law, Brigadier Jedediah Preble. Bangs mentioned at the time that the island contained 215 acres. Incidentally, Bangs also acquired several other islands before his death on May 23, 1762. Jedediah Preble now came into possession of Cushing Island. His son, the illustrious Commodore Edward Preble, known by many as the father of the American Navy, was the next owner.

Simon Skillings, called by Mabel Rogers Holt a person "sounding like a character out of Dickens," moved into Cushing's old home around the turn of the century, and gradually bought up six sevenths of Cushing Island, with Preble's heirs still holding on to the remaining one seventh in 1823.

Thirty-five years later, Canadian-born Lemuel Cushing, fourth cousin to Ezekiel Cushing, purchased the entire island. Constructing a hotel of brick high on the headland he named it the Ottawa House. A great attraction for Canadians, it was filled to overflowing every summer, but a fire destroyed the hotel in 1886.

Cushing was anxious to rebuild the hotel but didn't have enough money. He was forced to sell stock for the new edifice, which was put up at a cost of $75,000. A few years later Cushing sold his interest for $16,000. In 1917 the second hotel caught fire, burned to the ground and was never rebuilt. The First World War, which reached America that year, sounded the death knell of hotels and leisurely summer vacations as our fathers and grandfathers knew them.

Just before the beginning of the present century, Spring Point on Cushing Island was chosen as the site of Fort Christopher Levett. The twelve-inch guns of the fort were fired during the two world wars, and the long three-hundred-foot tunnel attracted almost every island visitor. Today, however, the defenses have lapsed into obsolescence.

Earlier this year I talked with Edith Burgess, wife of care-taker Herman Burgess. She told me that the island is privately owned by the Cushing Island Associates, an organization formed a generation ago. The Burgesses, both husband and wife, have been caretakers at Cushing Island for seven years, and are the only year-round residents at Cushing Island. Eleven of the island homes on the fort side of Cushing Island have been renovated and are privately owned. One of the buildings was a hospital and another a jail.

There are two piers on the island, both kept in excellent condition. The summer residents arrive at the island from Widgery Wharf in Portland aboard the *Marjorie Ann*, a craft which carries twenty-one people.*

For our final thought on Cushing Island we return to the occasion several generations ago when Senator Thomas Reed spoke from the veranda of the Ottawa House:

"Whoever stands here on a clear summer day . . . will find his eyes resting on a scene which for loveliness and varied beauty has no superior and perhaps no parallel on the broad earth. The long slope of grassy verdure, varied by the darker foliage of the trees, spreads to the water's edge. Then begins the bright sparkle of the summer sea, that many-twinkling smile of ocean, that countless laughter of the waves which has lighted up the heart of man centuries since Aeschylus died and centuries before he lived.

"Across the sunlit waters dotted with white sails or seamed with the bubbly foam of steamers' tracks, past the wharves bristling with masts and noisy with commerce, the gaze falls upon the houses sloping gently upward in the center and becoming more and more embowered with trees as they climb the hills. Altogether a scene which mingles all that is best and brightest of sea and shore."

*Family names of summer visitors to the island include Thaxter, Farrar, Meacham, Hammond, Quinn, Cole, Hitchcock, Hale, and Gignoux.

11

Ragged Island

When I landed at Ragged Island some years ago by canoe, I recalled a statement which Margaret Burr Todd made to me to the effect that the island was called Rugged Island on the early charts of the area, and it could still be called by that name today.

As of June 1972, six individuals or groups were listed as owning or being residents of the island.

The fifty-odd acres of Ragged Island are surrounded by White Bull Island, Little Bull Ledge, Round Rock, and Bald Dick Ledge. Ragged Island has the tiniest of harbors, and although settlements did not start there in the early days, there were plenty of wooden frames or flakes where fish were dried in the eighteenth century period. There is a Ghost Cliff on the western side of the island, which is nicely matched by a Devil's Wall some hundreds of yards away.

Elijah Kellogg, who called the island Elm Island in his many books, is one of two writers associated with Ragged Island, the other being Rockland-born poet Edna St. Vincent Millay, who lived at the island during the summer season, but at a later period than Kellogg.* Had the Reverend Mr. Kellogg and Miss Millay been able to meet at far-flung Ragged Island, they would have had much to say to each other, states Margaret Burr Todd.

Unfortunately, the boy of today hardly hears of the Reverend Elijah Kellogg, although in his prime, at least in the state of Maine, he outrivaled the well-known Horatio Alger, Jr., a Harvard graduate and another minister, who wrote more than a hundred books for boys.

Kellogg really has become part of Harpswell regional history. Born in 1813, he went to sea at thirteen, and later chronicled his experiences in several of his books. After preparing for the ministry at the Andover Theological Seminary, Kellogg was appointed pastor of the Harpswell Congregational Church in 1844. He built a house for his mother and himself at Harpswell on the eastern shore of Maquoit Bay in 1849, laboriously transporting field stones for the foundation and timber for the building to the mainland from Ragged Island. Three years later his mother died.

In 1854 Kellogg married Miss Hannah Pomery, a schoolmate of his at Gorham Academy. That same year he accepted the call of the Seaman's Friend Society in Boston. He became pastor of the Mariner's Church there and served as chaplain of the Boston Sailors' Home.

Kellogg's many stories for boys, which include the series on Elm Island, the first of which came out around 1876, were extremely popular. He not only was a very energetic and imaginative author, but was high-spirited as well, and possessed the talent to appeal to the boy of his period. Despite his success, his publishers failed in business, and Kellogg returned to Maine a poor man.

He preached at the Topsham Church until 1889, the year he

*Rockland is also the birthplace of actress Maxine Elliot, She was courted unsuccessfully by my father in the year 1881.

returned to his former position at Harpswell Church. There he served as pastor until his death on March 17, 1904. His funeral was held in the church two days later.

Elijah Kellogg's stories even today give the reader thrills about Elm Island, the Ghost Cliff, and Pleasant Cove. I am disappointed that most of the encyclopedias of the present age completely ignore him, but it is reassuring to know that the Boston Athenaeum has many of his publications. On the shelves of the Athenaeum I have examined his *Ark of Elm Island*, *Boy Farmers of Elm Island*, and *Charlie Bell, the Waif of Elm Island*, three of his many volumes concerning Ragged Island. Including reprints, there are in Boston libraries about twenty of his volumes. Boys of today cannot obtain his books easily, but they are available from libraries.

During our canoe trip in 1963 I was anxious to land at Ragged Island, knowing Mrs. Snow's interest in Edna St. Vincent Millay's poem *Renascence*, which she read in chapel at Rockford College in Illinois during her college years. The rain, wind, and waves prevented our landing at the island, however, as during the final hours of our journey we were concerned about getting back to the mainland. It was not until several years later that I finally reached my goal.

Edna St. Vincent Millay, who loved Ragged Island, was born in 1891. When she was nineteen years of age she composed the poem with which we will always identify her. Nothing in Edna St. Vincent Millay's later writing brought back the supreme thoughts in her *Renascence*. Her sonnets, which were published in one volume during Miss Millay's fiftieth year, range from Elizabethan rhetoric to contemporary "plain speaking." She became thoughtful of the future in the twenty-ninth year of her life, offering in her disillusionment the fears of inevitable old age and death.

In 1923 she was awarded the Pulitzer Prize. Shortly after that she married Eugen Jan Boissevain and set up housekeeping in the Berkshire Hills of Massachusetts.

Edna St. Vincent Millay went to Ragged Island almost every year during the prime of her life. Without question she deeply loved the Maine Coast.

12

Peak's Island

Just as Portland is the metropolis for most of Maine, so in a sense is Peak's Island the headquarters for all the islands in the Casco Bay region off the shores of South Portland. Historian Herbert Jones tells us that the first settlers here were of good sturdy stock made up mostly "of fishermen and those who go down to the sea in ships." They bore such typical Maine names as Trefethen, Welch, Parsons, Sterling, Jones, Woodbury, and Waite.

Going back through the years we find that one family owned a portion of Peak's Island from the days of the Indians, and only recently relinquished it. In the earliest times, Peak's Island was known as Pond Island, and this may succeed in confusing anyone, because at the present moment there are eight islands in Maine identified by the name of Pond.

When George Cleeves presented Peak's Island to Michael Mitton, it became Mitton's Island. At the time Munjoy owned it, his name identified the island; but when Munjoy's son-in-law Palmer took it at Munjoy's death, the title became Palmer's Island. Samuel Peak is said to have been the person for whom the island was finally named, but historian William Willis does not definitely state that fact for some reason.

During the Revolution there were only three houses standing on Peak's Island, and one day British troops went ashore and entertained the children living there with a bagpipe serenade which the children never forgot. This was all the music or entertainment at Peak's Island for several generations, but by the middle of the nineteenth century, when summer picnic grounds became popular, Peak's career as an amusement center began. We know that long before the 1850's Peak's Island was a well-patronized summer boarding area. Open-air bowling alleys were in business shortly after the middle of the century. Quoting a historian of the period, "the clatter of pins being hit by bowling balls often mingled with the sound of waves breaking on the rocky shores."

It was in 1850, however, according to Herbert Jones, that the summer resort business really began on Peak's Island. Before any other island could offer similar favors, William Jones turned his home into a reception building for summer guests, and soon he was serving the best of shore dinners. When the Grand Trunk Railroad opened a terminal over in Portland, scores of Canadians began the custom of visiting Peak's on almost every summer boat. In 1851, realizing the need for a fast steamer, Horatio G. Cook put the *Antelope* into service.

By the year 1880 Peak's could have been called the Coney Island of Maine. A huge barrel-shaped building on the island was first known as the Forest City Skating Rink, but later became the Gem Theater.

Greenwood Park, located fairly close to the theater, soon was known all over Maine. Vaudeville shows were given outdoors here, and balloonist Prince Leo was soon a favorite to thousands. He often ascended with his balloon many hundreds of feet in the air, then leaped from the vehicle, opened his parachute, and floated down to earth at Peak's Island.

It is said that Prince Leo never missed hitting the island, thus bettering the record of an aerial performer from Massachusetts, Lauriat, who often jumped from his balloon over the park at Nahant, Massachusetts. One fine July 4 in the 1830's Lauriat made his leap but missed Nahant and landed out to sea. He was rescued, however.

During the 1890's Professor Oldwie gave a really startling performance at Peak's when, wearing his specially constructed floating shoes, he walked on the water! This feat had first been accomplished by Peter Falcon during the building of the world-famous Minot's Light off the South Shore near Boston. He built two great oblong-shaped platforms of crude rubber which gave him enough displacement and buoyancy to walk along on the ocean's surface in a manner similar to that which the skiers of today use to make progress on level snow areas.

It was at the time of the Spanish-American War in 1898 that manager Bart McCullum decided to turn the Forest City Skating Rink into the Gem Theater. He hired Byron Douglas as participating director of the various light musical shows, which soon attracted great attention. For twenty-five cents one had a round trip to the island and a ticket to the current show, but for special seats another quarter had to be paid. Players of the period included Charlotte Hunt, Scott Cooper, T. Lester Wallack, Robert Lowe, William Canfield, and Edward Poland.

At times, I have been told, during rather warm evenings, the canvas sides of the theater were rolled up to permit "the wafting of cool breezes off the ocean." Then the fascinated audiences were able to watch, in real sea-breeze comfort, such plays as *The Midnight Express, All the Comforts of Home, The Mail Girl, London by Midnight,* and *Diplomacy.*

Almost every night in the summertime there was a display of fireworks, with a realistic naval battle the high point of the evening's illumination. Bart McCullum gained a reputation all over Maine by producing new plays and presenting talent that would later make the grand circuit on Broadway. As the master of ceremonies at Peak's, McCullum carried out his programs in a manner similar to the summer stock theaters of today on Cape Cod and in other parts of New England. It is impossible to estimate the numbers of drama lovers who went to Peak's Island at the height of the summer season, but the steamers *Forest City, Greenwood, S.S. Spring, Emita,* and *Forest Queen* were required to transport the crowds.

I wish I had the ability to take the reader back into the carnival days that Peak's Island enjoyed between the years 1870 and 1910, before the automobile became important on the mainland. Activities of every type were provided on the island. Roller polo games, boat carnivals, operas, musical shows, dancing, skating—all were enjoyed. I have been told that there was a women's band that at times played to enraptured watchers, but I cannot find a record of this elusive organization at Peak's Island in any source book I have examined. Such a band did play on the mainland at Riverton Park.

The most famous shipwreck associated with Peak's Island was that of the schooner *Helen Eliza,* lost in the terrible gale of September 8, 1869. During that storm the craft accompanying the *Helen Eliza,* the *Yankee Girl,* vanished utterly, and neither she nor any member of her crew was ever seen again. The *Helen Eliza* herself went ashore at the south end of Peak's, and was dashed to pieces in a short time. Her captain, Edward J. Millett, and ten of the eleven crew members were lost. The only one to save himself was Charles Jordan, a man more than fortunate, for on not one but two previous occasions Jordan had been the sole survivor of a particular incident or accident. Confined in Libby Prison during the Civil War, he alone out of a company of eighty lived to return home, and when in 1867 the schooner *Day* was lost off Cape Cod, he was the only one saved from a crew of thirty. Interviewed after the wreck of the *Helen Eliza,* Jordan gave the details of the disaster. Here in his own words is the story of what happened.

*   *   *

"During the latter part of the forenoon of the 8th inst., the weather looked threatening, and Capt. Millett concluded to run into Portland harbor. The first land made was Ram Island, about a mile outside of White Head. During the latter part of the afternoon a thick fog set in, which was followed by a perfect deluge of rain, and the wind increased until it blew a regular hurricane.

"Both anchors were let go, but the cables parted, and the vessel was put under short sail. The gale increased fearfully, and the jib was blown clean out of the bolt-ropes. Saw Portland Light, which we undertook to run for, but were too far to the eastward to strike the channel.

"There was no earthly help for us now. With both anchors gone, the wind blowing a hurricane, and a tremendous sea running, there was but little doubt that the vessel would go ashore at Peak's Island, and, in that event, the chances of being saved were slim indeed. The prospect was a gloomy one, but the crew were undaunted, and resolved to do their best. Capt. Millett stood at his post of duty at the helm, to the very last moment, and in all probability received his death-blow from the main boom.

"After running some twenty minutes, the thumping of the vessel's bottom gave evidence that the critical time was near at hand. She did not stop in her course, but kept moving. I went into the forecastle and stripped myself of everything but my shirt and pants for the coming trial. I had hardly done so when the vessel struck heavily, smashing in the bow, instantly killing five persons who were with me. I immediately ran into the hold, when a tremendous sea knocked off the deck, and I was swept into the raging waters.

"I seemed, as if by intuition, to at once realize my position, and being a good swimmer, I made for the wreck, which I reached, and clinging to it, regained my breath and got rested. Seeing an empty barrel floating near, I let go my hold of the wreck, and was fortunate enough to secure it. Placing my breast upon the head, I forced the empty portion under water. This served as a great support, and with it I attempted to effect a landing.

"The waves ran fearfully high, and as I was borne along I passed George W. Clark and Benjamin Lurvey, two of my shipmates, who were clinging to a plank. If ever in my life I desired company, it was at this critical time; but prudence whispered that I must not make myself known, for if I did the chances of escape of all three of us would be rendered far more hazardous. I heard them each speak of their fearful position, and doubting whether they should be able to hold on; and the last words I heard them utter was a promise that if either was saved, they would tell the folks at home the full particulars.

"It now required my utmost efforts to keep the barrel in position, as the undertow was very powerful, but I managed to do so, and soon saw a ledge of rocks. To effect a landing amid the surf as it beat against its sides, without being injured, was a dangerous task. The waves at one time heaving me toward the ledge, then retreating, would engulf me in their treacherous grasp, threatening every moment to bury me beneath the water. But by the help of my barrel I succeeded, and inserting my fingers in the crevices of the rocks, commenced the toilsome passage up their jagged sides, reaching the top completely exhausted.

"While resting, I heard the voice of Clark, who was hailing some one. I answered the call, telling him where he was, and enjoining upon him to hold on and try to get upon the ledge. I did not hear him again, and probably the two men were instantly swallowed up in the undertow.

"I soon found that the ledge did not form a part of the island, but was covered at high water, and, as the tide was coming in, I knew that I was not yet out of danger. After a little time I again plunged into the seething waters. Another terrible conflict with the surf followed, in which it seemed impossible for me to make any headway, as my strength was fast failing.

"Words are inadequate to describe such a situation. Moments seemed like hours, and the sullen roar of the waters as they beat upon the rocks was an awful accompaniment. I neared the shore, the dim outline of which I saw, and making one desperate effort, was fortunate in effecting a landing and in getting myself out of reach of the breakers.

"It was now about nine o'clock in the evening, and the exertions of the past two hours began to tell upon me fearfully. I could scarcely lift one foot before the other, but I persevered and emerged into a pathway which led me to a house. It proved to be the residence of Mr. Smith Hadlock. The inmates were at once aroused, and were unremitting in their attentions, furnishing me with a suit of clothing, and doing everything in their power for my comfort.

"As soon as I had partaken of refreshments and got rested, I accompanied a party of men belonging on the island, in search for the bodies of my shipmates. Mr. Jones, landlord of the hotel on Peak's Island, was unremitting in his attentions, and secured for me a free passage home. The inhabitants of the island, mostly poor fishermen, made me up a purse of $18, and, while in the depot at Portland, $11 was raised in my behalf. The Mayor of the city sought me out, and was also very kind."

For years many people have mistakenly associated the *Helen Eliza* disaster with Henry Wadsworth Longfellow's ballad, "The Wreck of the Hesperus." As Longfellow wrote the poem in 1839, he could not possibly have based it on the wreck of the *Helen Eliza* which did not take place until thirty years later. "The Wreck of the Hesperus" actually was inspired by the loss of the Wiscasset schooner *Favorite*.

Index